D1826507

A return to Greece and to Kos in the Cyclades sets John Ebdon on a fresh round of adventures – funny, sad, ridiculous and poignant.

This book, like *Ebdon's Odyssey*, is about people: The Proper Young Woman and Knickers-to-Match, who invade his midnight accordion music or disturb his musings at the Taverna, and also the islanders Stephano, the irrepressible lecher, the long-suffering Klimi and the indomitable Mama Barbunia.

JOHN EBDON

Ebdon's Iliad

Illustrations by
Nicola Jennings

London
UNWIN PAPERBACKS
Boston   Sydney

First published in Great Britain by Heinemann/Peter Davies Ltd, 1983
First published by Unwin Paperbacks 1984

UNWIN® PAPERBACKS
40 Museum Street, London WC1A 1LU, UK

Unwin Paperbacks
Park Lane, Hemel Hempstead, Herts HP2 4TE, UK

George Allen & Unwin Australia Pty Ltd
8 Napier Street, North Sydney, NSW 2060, Australia

© John Ebdon 1983, 1984

ISBN 0 04 910078 5

Reproduced, printed and bound in Great Britain by
Hazell Watson & Viney Limited,
Member of the BPCC Group,
Aylesbury, Bucks

TO
GEORGE AND ANNA-MARIE ZAGORIANOS,
MY FRIENDS IN THE ISLANDS
OF
RHODES AND KARPATHOS
AND
'MARIA'

ΣΤΟΥΣ
ΓΙΩΡΓΟ ΚΑΙ ΑΝΝΑ-ΜΑΡΙΑ ΖΑΓΟΡΙΑΝΟΥ
ΣΤΟΥΣ ΦΙΛΟΥΣ ΜΟΥ ΣΤΑ ΝΗΣΙΑ
ΡΟΔΟΥ ΚΑΙ ΚΑΡΠΑΘΟΥ
ΚΑΙ ΣΤΗΝ
'ΜΑΡΙΑ'

Contents

Illustrations

Acknowledgements

Timsway Travel
Triton Holidays, Rhodes
Small World

Introduction

'I CANNOT UNDERSTAND *why*,' wrote a plaintive woman from Wokingham after reading the accounts of my adventures in *Ebdon's Odyssey*, 'but *nothing* like that happened to *me* when *I* was in Greece. *And*,' she added, continuing to italicize, '*I* stayed for three weeks. In the *Aphrodite*. . .' I replied politely, but succinctly. 'Madam,' I wrote, 'I can.' And I could. Only too well. One does not see the true face of Greece from a large hotel in Athens or any other city.

Such places are not of my world. Nor are the tourist orientated islands and resorts. Deservedly they are popular. In them the hedonists find Paradise; but they learn little or nothing about Greek life; or the Greeks. Which is why I avoid them. My milieu in Greece is one of tavernas, simple pensions and unsophisticated people. The former have opened their doors to me and the latter, their hearts; and by so doing, have placed me for ever in their debt.

This book is about them – the indigenous among whom I stayed; and the visitors who entered my life, albeit briefly, whilst I did so: Knickers-to-Match was one such person; and his wife was another. I met them in the island of Karpathos. Neither was easy to forget. . . .

One last particular. Unlike the *Iliad* of Homer this story is not a tale of tragedies and trials. But there is pathos as well as bathos within it, and tears besides laughter; but these are the ingredients of life. And particularly life in the Isles of Greece.

Vasili

I WAS LISTENING to a recording of the St Matthew Passion when the telephone rang on a Maundy Thursday evening in 1980. It was a long distance call from a friend in Kardamena.

I said: 'Good Lord, what a marvellous surprise! How lovely to hear you – how are you?' 'Splendid,' she said, 'fine. And you?' 'Cold,' I said, 'and missing Greece – horribly!' And laughed. 'Anyway, what's the news? How is everybody?'

'Well, I –'

'How's Athena?'

'Athena? Oh she's pregnant.'

'What again?'

'Uh huh. She's bought a new washing machine on the strength of it.'

'Bravo! And Debbi? Still flouncing and flirting around the yoghurt and pastries?'

'Not exactly – she's pregnant too. Getting married next month.'

'My goodness, it has been a busy winter. Never a dull

moment by the sound of it. And Kosta?'

'Oh, still hard at backgammon and being beastly to Anastasi.'

'The bastard! And Vasili – how's dear old Vasili?'

There was a small silence at the other end of the line.

'Well,' she said, 'actually that's why I'm phoning.' And paused again.

'You see,' she said, and cleared her throat, 'you see, he died. Yesterday.'

The line from Kos was very clear but I heard little of what she said after that. I echoed her goodbye, replaced the receiver and walked slowly into the sitting room. The majesty of Bach's Passion was still coming through the speakers. Christ had called from the Cross and now the sweet melancholy of the chorale filled the room.

> 'Wenn ich einmal soll scheiden
> So scheide nicht von mir.'

'When once I must depart,' they sang, 'do not depart from me. . .'

Gently the oboes and the strings died away and there was a click as the stylus came to the end of the record and swung back to its place. Mechanically I took the disc from the turntable, returned it to its sleeve and put it in the rack: then I poured myself a drink and sat down to think.

Gradually the reality sank in. Vasili was dead. Vasili, sailor and fisherman who could have been the prototype for Hemingway's *Old Man of the Sea*, who knew the stars over Kos and the island's waters like the back of his calloused hands, Vasili who had dedicated much of his adult life to emptying most of the Dodecanese of all forms of alcohol and with whom I had spent countless hours in small tavernas learning bad Greek and worse table manners, Vasili, my friend and mentor, was dead.

The warmth from my hand had clouded the glass with condensation. Contemplatively I stirred the martini around the melting ice and gazed for a while in silence at a photograph on a side table. From the stern of his fishing boat and perched on the gunwale with one strong hand on the tiller, Vasili smiled back at me – a wiry man in his early sixties with close-cropped hair and a clipped moustache. His face was the colour of mahogany and lined like a relief map of the Irrawaddy. 'Maimounaki' I used to call him – 'little monkey'. And with the addition of a red pill-box hat he would not have been out of place on the top of a barrel-organ.

I sipped at my drink, remembering when I had taken the picture. It was on a blue and white September day with skies the colour of the Greek flag. We had chugged along the coast from the village of Kardamena towards the headland of Kephalos singing together over the noise of the engine and eating huge red slices of water melon. We were stickily content.

Two miles from Kardamena the engine spluttered and died abruptly as the propeller stopped turning. Vasili swore and spat out a mouthful of pips to the fishes. 'Sheet!' he said drawing on his limited English vocabulary acquired from the Royal Navy, 'Sheetenboogerdamn!'; and presenting his ample bottom to the heavens, leaned over the side.

His muffled voice came to me from near the sea's face. 'There is,' he shouted, returning to the richness of his mother tongue and choosing his words with care, 'an * * * something round the * * * * screw.' Minutes later triumphantly he staggered to his feet clutching a twisted pair of faded directoire knickers.

Vasili held them at arm's length and opened them out. Once turquoise and no doubt cherished by a lady of singularly generous proportions, patently they had suffered from their long immersion; but it said much for the manufacturer that they were still whole and retained some elasticity. As one playing a hornpipe on a concertina Vasili tested the waistband between his outstretched arms and the sodden knickers danced before him in convulsive jerks. He eyed them approvingly and squeezed them out. 'Bravo!' he said. And hung them up to dry. Vasili was a thrifty man and allowed little to go to waste.

It was a happy day. Successfully we fished off Kephalos with hand lines, drank two or three ouzos in the beach taverna there and returned without incident to Kardamena with the now dry knickers fluttering brazenly against the setting sun. Vasili unhooked them from the mast, put them in a blue polythene bag; and added the fish. 'Endaxi,' he said as he patted them into place – 'ke tora parme sto spithi mu – ne?' 'Yes,' I said, 'Why not – let's go to your house'. 'Ne,' he nodded. 'And there we shall drink some more ouzo and some retsina and eat the fishes. Ella – come!'

Like its owner, Vasili's house smacked of the sea. Indeed, going into the Vasili ménage was not unlike entering Poseidon's grotto, for throughout it was decorated liberally with the fruits of the Aegean which, over the years, had found their way into Vasili's nets. The living room, painted sea-green and used only on special occasions, was the pièce de résistance.

On a sideboard, fan-shaped sponges stood between photographs of daughters whose unions had been blessed, those who might produce and one of whose fertility there was no doubt at all, bunches of dried seaweed and petrified

The knickers fluttered brazenly.

driftwood hung from the ceiling, patinated urns, limpet-encrusted stone jars and bottles stood in corners, scallop-shell ashtrays littered a dining table graced with a centrepiece of an exquisite five-stemmed branch of coral; and from a shelf near the window the glued remains of a one-eyed crab, its claws open in a stiff gesture of welcome, gazed unseeingly at a nest of adjacent sea-urchins. It was a setting in which it would have come as no surprise had Vasili's wife Poppi appeared waving a trident and balancing uncertainly on a fish tail.

That evening she was installed in the place reserved for all Greek housewives. By the sink. Sewing. Amply built, she was a dear dumpy lady with a sallow complexion who put me much in mind of an overweight boxer dog, a Disney creation, warm and cuddly with puckered features. 'Ah,' she said mournfully as we entered, 'Ahh;' and eased herself from her chair. 'Ah,' she reiterated, setting down the trousers she was repairing, 'Ti kanete Yanni – how are you?' 'Kala,' I said, 'fine.' 'Poli kala,' Vasili emphasized, 'poli.' And tipped the fishes into the sink. 'These,' he pronounced, 'are for the meal and these,' he said reaching into the bag and extracting the knickers with the air of a conjuror producing a rabbit from a hat – 'are for you!'

Momentarily Poppi stared at them with sad brown eyes. Then, taking them from him and holding them dubiously between fingers and thumbs she raised them toward the naked bulb in the ceiling. 'Ahh,' she said; and assessed their adjustability. Certainly they seemed right for size. 'Endaxi?' asked Vasili, and without waiting for an answer went in search of a bottle.

For an hour Vasili and I sat in the vine-covered patio drinking ouzo among the blue-painted olive oil cans planted with basil and fennel and rosemary. Beyond the wrought-iron gate under the concrete arch leading to the street, two women had a slanging match. Face to face like two she-cats, higher and higher their voices rose, raucous and rusty, nose to nose, then drawing apart they continued to spit their loaded insults through the night as backwards they went their separate ways.

Vasili chuckled into his ouzo. 'O! po! po!' he said as the diatribe died, 'Mana mu! That was Thespe and Maria – they both want the same man. They've been at it for years. And they're both over sixty! But there Yanni mu, ine e zoi – it is life!' He chuckled again and drained his glass. 'Thank God,' he said, 'that I'm happy with Poppi and she with me. Another ouzo, ne?'

That they were happy was indisputable. In their own simple undemanding ways they loved each other dearly. Each knew their place and accepted their allotted roles in true island fashion. His obligation was to provide and protect. Her duty was to bear children; to cook and look after the house; and to turn a blind eye to his extravagances. It was not for her to question the hours he spent in tavernas and cafeneons with his cronies, drinking or playing backgammon: what he did in his leisure time was his affair. It is a man's world in the Dodecanese.

In the kitchen the object of his affection hummed untunefully to an oscillating transistor while she cooked the fishes and soon the smell of frying reached us through the open door.

'Bravo!' said Vasili, patting his stomach in anticipation as we went in, and disappeared through some red curtains which separated the kitchen from a bedroom. Behind them came the sound of heavy snoring. There was a clang as somewhere in the darkness beyond, Vasili shut a refrigerator door, and simultaneously there was a break in the sleeper's rhythm. Three short snorts followed by a long plaintive exhalation indicated that his subconscious had been violated.

'Dimitri,' said Vasili as he reappeared carrying two bottles of retsina; and tapped his forehead significantly. 'Ah yes,' I said, 'of course. Dimitri.' 'Ah yes,' intoned Poppi crossing herself and taking a fish, 'Dimitri. Our small problem. Kali orexi – good appetite!' Deftly she removed the dorsal fin with her fingers and holding the fish by the head and tail, sank her teeth into it. 'Kala!' she said approvingly as the flesh came cleanly away from the spine, 'poli kala – very good.' And stripped its belly. Beyond the curtain Dimitri laughed in his sleep. Poppi looked up apprehensively from the skeleton. 'Aah,' she said, 'Dimitri.' And demolished the head.

Dimitri was her brother, a man whom the charitable would describe as simple and the more pedantic as potty. However, both parties would agree unreservedly that he was not an asset to Kardamena. Particularly during the tourist season. Of indeterminate years, he wore a shiny black hat with ear-flaps, murky green mittens, and a fixed grin. He possessed but one tooth shaped like a mushroom stalk, a formidable number of idiosyncrasies and a well-worn zip to his trousers. That it did show signs of unfair wear and tear was understandable, for prominent among his quirks was a tendency to raise his hat, bid one good morning, good afternoon or good evening as the hour dictated – and then expose himself. He was not good for trade. It was just before ten o'clock that he provided the cabaret.

Apart from the sound of Vasili working his way through his seventh fish there was little noise in the room.

The tired batteries of the transistor had petered out, a replete Poppi, her elbows on the table and a pile of carcasses before her was reflectively picking her teeth with a bone; and Dimitri had stopped snoring. It was the calm before the storm.

Outside a night-bird called and as it cried, so the red plush curtains parted. 'Kalispera si olus,' said Dimitri as he emerged through them in the manner of a theatre manager announcing an hiatus in the programme, 'Good evening everybody!' And did his party piece.

Vasili glanced at him over the fish. 'Yasu,' he muttered and reached for another. Undismayed by his inability to stop the traffic on this occasion and no doubt consoling himself with thoughts of his success at the day's matinée performance, Dimitri leered happily at us, replaced his props and retired back stage. 'Ha-ha-ha!' he cackled, 'ha-ha-ha!' At the other end of the table Poppi cupped her face in her hands and gave a low moan. 'Thenbarazi,' said Vasili pushing his plate away and sucking his fingers, 'michi rotora – it could be worse. Think what he did on Thursday. . .'

And so the memories of that autumn day of long ago washed over me. It seemed an age now since the telephone had rung and in the small hours of Good Friday the room had become cold. I put my half-finished glass aside and took another long look at the photograph. It was unbelievable that I would not see him again.

One by one I turned out the lights and prepared for bed. I said a prayer for Vasili's soul but wondered what I would say to Poppi when next I saw her in the coming October. It would, I thought, be an emotional reunion.

CHAPTER I

Kardamena Revisited

M Y MEETING WITH Poppi was traumatic. In my poor Greek I had written to her that I would be coming but she was not at home when I called upon her early on that October Friday morning. She was, so a neighbour told me outside the gate of her house, at the church. Perhaps if I went there I would find her: certainly she had had my letter and was expecting me. 'Epharisto,' I said, 'thank you;' and began to walk the short distance towards it.

She was on her way back to the house when I met her. Dressed in her widow's weeds and moving arthritically down the narrow street which led from the church and with her head bowed, she looked much smaller than when I had last seen her.

I shouted: 'Poppi!' and she stopped in her tracks. 'Ahh,' she said, and called my name, her face puckering. Then, breaking into a run she stumbled towards me her arms outstretched, threw herself into my open arms and cried her heart out. 'Yanni, Yanni, Yanni,' she sobbed, 'why, why, why – in the name of Christ, sweet Jesus, why?'

I never thought a woman could hold so many tears.

For a while I held her against me until her immediate grief was spent, silently adding my own tears to hers. God knows, I too had loved the man. Then, with my arm about her shoulders, slowly we walked back.

Vasili, she told me, had had an operation and a blood transfusion in Athens. There had been no trouble and within a week he was back in Kardamena, happy and well she thought. Two days later he died – suddenly. The local doctor had been very kind, but she had not really understood his explanation. Perhaps, she said, it was bad blood that Vasili had been given but she did not know. And in any case it did not matter. Her Vasili was dead and that is what mattered.

The gate was ajar when we reached the house. Dimitri had returned. He was sitting in a wicker chair, holding a fly swat and staring vacantly into space through tinted glasses. I said: 'Yasu Dimitri,' and held out my hand. Ignoring it he looked at me uncomprehendingly. 'Ti?' he said, 'What?' He did not remember me.

'I'm Yanni,' I said, and paused. 'I'm sorry about Vasili.'

His eyes flickered behind the darkened lenses. 'Vasili?' he said, and blinked again. 'Oh yes, Vasili. He's dead you know.' And smacked at a fly. 'They gave me this because he's dead – he's dead and so they gave me this.' He pointed to his black arm band. 'That means he's dead,' he said.

Poppi started to cry again, quietly this time, and touched my elbow. 'Ella,' she said, and opened the door to the sitting room. 'Come,' she repeated and I followed her through.

Inside it was still and airless and there was a stale smell and a feeling of emptiness for which at first I could not account but which soon became apparent. The room had been stripped of all Vasili's possessions. Sponges, corals, driftwood, shells – all had been removed. On the sideboard, a large black-draped picture of Vasili formed the centre of a montage of photographs while others of him lay face upwards in front of them, each on a cushion of black. And pinned diagonally across the dining table now innocent of ornament, was a broad black band of crêpe. There are no half measures when the Greeks mourn.

For a while we stood there side by side, wrapped in our thoughts and a blanket of silence. Outside there was a thwack and a high pitched laugh as Dimitri swatted another fly. 'Pende!' he shrilled, 'five – that's five!'

Poppi caught her breath and clutched her handkerchief to her mouth. Once more I put my arm around her and she rested her head against my chest. She stayed so for a moment or two and then gave a little sigh like an exhausted child at the end of a tearful day. 'Sighnomi,' she said, 'I'm sorry.' She dabbed at her eyes and went into the kitchen.

I sat with her for an hour or so eating raw wild artichokes and sipping ice-cold nero vroichinos – delicious pure rainwater drawn from a well. It was like drinking life itself. Then at noon I took my leave.

'You'll come again?' she asked as we embraced in the doorway.

'Of course,' I said, 'I shall be here for a week.' 'Kala,' she said, 'good.' And stroked my arm in the way of all Greek women. 'Perhaps you will come with me to see his grave, ne? It has a very beautiful stone – white marble, Yanni, and soon it will have his name on it – a man from Kos will come to make his name.' She wrote the characters in the air with her forefinger. 'Vasili Chrystopoulos,' she said, 'in big letters: and his photograph. Ine poli orea, ne – very beautiful, yes?' 'Poli,' I said, quietly, 'very.' She looked at me and her eyes started to fill again. 'Yasu Yanni mu,' she said, and turning quickly away from me went inside.

Dimitri was still in his chair by the wall, staring at a pile of dead flies on the table before him. The iron gate squealed on its hinges as I opened it and he looked up at me, edentate and gormless, a Brueghel peasant.

'Vasili's in the necrotophia, isn't he,' he said. I nodded. Slowly he moved his head in mute agreement with me. 'Ne,' he repeated, 'in the cemetery. He's dead.' And looked down at the flies again. 'Like these,' he said, 'just . . . like . . . these. . .'

I clanged the gate shut behind me and left him to his poor idiot thoughts. Much of Poppi's grief had brushed off on me and I felt sapped and a little depressed: life, I thought as I lit my pipe, would not be easy for her during the coming months.

I threw the match away and after a few yards I turned left into the main street and started to walk towards my pension. It had been very late and dark when I had arrived by taxi from Kos the previous night and I had seen nothing of the village. I had supped with Kosta the grocer with whom I was staying, drunk some retsina with mutual friends and gone to bed. Now, in the midday humidity of St Dimitri's Little Summer and after a year's absence I began to take stock.

The long narrow street was bustling with tourists – shopping, eating, hiring mopeds, bleating, meeting, white and brown – French, Australians, Germans, British, Swiss and Swedes, all were there. Ahead of me, one of them, pink and sore, inquired plaintively of a travel representative what he should do about his prickly heat. 'Try calamine,' she said, and cycled off to shepherd her excursion party towards a waiting bus. 'That's the pink stuff,' said his skinning companion, 'it comes off on the sheets. And for Gawd's sake, Ron, stop scratching – you'll make them bleed.'

As I passed them on the periphery of argument and an uncomfortable day and even worse night to come, my mind went back three years to when there were few shops, no motor-bikes and I was one of ten visitors in Kardamena. Last year, I remembered, they came in their hundreds. Now daily they were landing by plane load at the nearby international airport.

A German family on cycles overtook me, weaving their ways with wobbling wheels and jangling bells through the oncoming pedestrian traffic and a quartet of ice-cream aficionados meandered towards me licking in concert at their melting cornets as I jostled past them. Outside a souvenir shop a superannuated Brünhilde appraised a tea-shirt emblazoned 'I love Kos'. Big buttocked and looking towards heaven for arithmetical guidance, quickly she converted the price tag into marks, shot approving eyebrows towards a peroxide hairline and then still muttering the figure, barged her way inside to make her purchase. Next door at the supermarket a close-cropped ginger-headed boy irritable with heat petulantly sucked his Pepsi through a straw and kicked his mother's ankle. She rounded on him sharply. 'Give over Shaun,' she snapped. And smacked his head. He was an objectionable child and should, I thought, have been put down at birth.

Glancing at him over my right shoulder and secretly sympathizing with the philosophy of the late King Herod, I sauntered on, hands deep in the pockets of my shorts, pondering on this changed Kardamena and then paused to relight my pipe in front of a shop window.

A quartet of ice cream aficionados meandered towards me.

It was an electrical store and one which in bygone days had presented a dim and dusty interior and an undistinguished collection of tangled cables, two-pin plugs and 40-watt light bulbs. These, together with a standard refrigerator, used to be displayed haphazardly behind unwashed glass; but as I saw, clearly the wind of change had blown through the establishment; and with gale force.

Freshly painted inside and out in cream and green, with concealed and spluttering fluorescent tubes buzzing like flies caught in cobwebs and alternately producing intermittent bursts of bright pink light and shadows, the window was filled with an impressive array of goods. Toasted-sandwich makers, food mixers and hair-driers, washing machines and freezers, all were represented and begging to be plugged in, unearthed, to waiting sockets.

There was also a large jagged hole in the centre of the plate glass.

Covered with a patch of blue polythene cut from a carrier bag and held in place with criss-crossed strips of sellotape, it marred the overall impression of prosperity and order and I wondered what had caused it. Certainly the glass chippings which lay like ice crystals inside at the base of the window suggested that the wound had been inflicted quite recently; but I was still musing on the possible reasons for the scar when I reached the end of the street and entered the village square.

To my right was the open sea and the jetty pointing towards the Datça peninsula of Turkey, hazy with heat in the distance. Tourists in twos and threes ambled along it, occasionally stopping to peer at the crews of fishing caïques at their moorings or at little boys who, stretched flat upon their stomachs, leaned over its edge fishing with hand lines baited with stale bread; before me across the square and backed by a blue-grey mass of mountain was Hotel Stelio. And outside it sitting at a table in the shade of a large umbrella, drinking coffee with his farmer cousin Yanni, was the man himself.

For Stelio, sitting and drinking coffee was a new-found luxury. When first he had welcomed me to the village late on a windswept and drizzling April night some three years past he was incapable of relaxing in any way. Daily at seven-thirty in the morning he drove the bus to Kos, did business in the town then drove it back in the early afternoon. He supervised the running of his small hotel, negotiated bookings, helped in the kitchen, served in his restaurant until late at night, checked the bills and charmed his guests. Annually, as Kardamena grew, so did his bank balance – and his duodenal ulcer – and the cost of his labours was etched on his face. Then, slowly, he began to ease up.

In 1979 I had had a letter from a mutual friend telling me that, 'Stelio had given up the bus.' And prior to my visit I had heard that he was running the restaurant no longer. Nor was there any reason why he should. His hotel commanded the best sea view in Kardamena and with the increasing growth of tourism it was sought eagerly by several travel firms each competing with the other. Stelio was assured of a full house – in all seasons. Also, with foresight and conjecturing that the large area of beach and land to the east of his hotel would in all probability be given up by the Greek army and opened to the public he was building two new houses near that beach. To let. Stelio was a businessman; and no fool.

Like most of the village, Stelio had known of my coming and we had met briefly and embraced in the street outside Kosta's shop the night before but no more than that. He would not come in to Kosta's to drink retsina; or anything else. Kosta was not his friend. And so we had parted with the promise that we would meet today. At his place.

It was Yanni, my namesake, who saw me first. 'Yanni!' he shrieked from under the umbrella, 'Yanni mu – yasu!' And jumping from his seat he ran towards me still shouting. 'Kalostone, kalostone!' he bellowed as we met in the centre of the square and kissed each other roundly as befits two men who share the same Name Day, 'Welcome! Welcome back!' 'It's good to be back,' I said, giving him a bear hug, and with our arms around each other we went over to join Stelio.

'Ah,' he said as he got up to greet us, 'now I can see you properly, now in the light I can see you better. Po! Po! Po! Yanni mu – you have put on weight! Ne, Yanni,' he said, patting my stomach, 'Yes, there is a child in there, I think. Sosta Yanni,' he inquired of his cousin, 'symphonis – you agree?' 'Ne,' said Farmer Yanni entering into the spirit of things, 'I agree, and any moment now. Bravo Yanni!'

'Epharisto,' I said, 'epharisto poli! Teliosate – have you finished?' 'And in any case,' I continued, addressing myself to Stelio and pointing to his own increased girth, 'I am not the only one!' 'Ah,' said Yanni, crossing himself, 'that is because the ulcer has gone, thanks be to the God!'

'The going of the ulcer has nothing to do with the God,' said Stelio who was a vehement agnostic, 'it is because I have less worry – it is worry which makes men thin!'

'And worms,' said Yanni, ever close to nature, 'do you remember Zachariah over at Pyli? He once had the wo –'

'Yes,' said Stelio impatiently, 'I remember, but –'

'And he became thin.'

'Yes! yes! I –'

9

'As a reed! And I recollect –'

'We all do.'

'That he wasted away and –'

'And died,' said Stelio.

'And died,' echoed Yanni.

'And has gone *back* to the worms.'

'But through their stomachs to *Heaven*!' cried Yanni triumphantly albeit with dubious theology and thumping upon the metal table, 'to heav –' 'Skoopithya!' shouted Stelio thumping back, 'rubbish! There is no heaven – paradise is in the purse!'

'Unbeliever!' screeched Yanni, whipping off his cap and hurling it to the ground. 'Dupe of the priests!' screamed Stelio waving his arms. 'Fools of the world!' I shouted on a rising cadence, 'would you murder each other for a worm?'

It was modern Greek drama at its best and I revelled in it. All the traits of the Greeks were displayed in that short scene. Exaggeration, histrionics and intensity, a quick loosing of emotions and then as suddenly, a dying of the flame.

'Mana mu!' said Stelio mopping his forehead, 'religion and politics and words, words, words. Now you know, Yanni, why democracy started in Greece! Lipon, kathiste – sit down. Coffee?'

For an hour we sat there, talking easily as old friends do despite the interruption of a year, and exchanging news. Stelio's brother had died, his daughter was engaged, Yanni's farm was doing well and he had built on to his house and was leasing rooms to a travel company. There was, he allowed, more money from that activity than from growing tomatoes and his apartments were always booked. He beamed at me across the table and rubbed his forefinger and thumb together. 'Poli drachma, Yanni. Katalavis? You understand? Plenty money!'

I nodded, 'Yes,' I said, 'I've noticed. And,' I added, thinking of the electrical shop in the particular, 'more goods on which to spend it. Dishwashers for example, and freezers.' 'Ne,' said Stelio, 'and now there is no need to go to Kos for such things. There is a store full of them here.' 'I know,' I said, 'I've seen it. It has a hole in the window.'

Stelio's eyes flickered. 'Ah, yes,' he said; and peered into his coffee. 'Of course. The hole.'

'Ah yes,' said Yanni massaging his face with an open hand, 'the hole.' And sniggered through his fingers.

Stelio swirled the remains of the coffee in the cup and drank it with a slurp. 'Yanni,' he said, setting the receptacle down in its stained saucer, 'do you want to know how the hole is coming?' 'Yes,' I said, 'I do. It puzzled me. Greatly.'

'Endaxi,' said Stelio, and disappeared into the foyer of his hotel. Moments later he reappeared, quickly crossed to the table, came to attention and placed an object on it.

It was an alarm clock. Innocent of glass with the second hand lurching drunkenly toward its fellow, it had a severe dent near the stop button and countless abrasions. It was not very well.

'This,' said Stelio picking it up and shaking it near his ear but failing to bring it back to life, 'is what caused the breaking. And can you think why?' I shook my head. 'Then,' said Stelio stubbing out his cigarette and lighting another, 'I will tell you.' 'Ne,' said Yanni cupping his chin in his hands and resting his elbows upon the table, 'we will *both* tell you.'

The story which unfolded contained all the ingredients of a Ben Travers farce, a touch of Euripedes and a soupçon of Sartre.

Once upon a time, or to be more precise a fortnight ago, a couple had stayed in the hotel celebrating as couples will, a wedding anniversary. And they did all the things that couples do on holiday in Greece. They lazed and bathed and wined and dined; and one fine night when the moon was high, they went to the disco; and they drank a very great deal.

It was in the small hours that the lovelight in their eyes grew dim. Possibly because his feet were killing him after several abortive attempts to master the intricacies of Greek dancing but probably because of his wife's readiness to accept tutorials in that art, the husband announced that he wished to leave. Quickly. With difficulty his wife disengaged herself from her immediate mentor, with even greater difficulty got her husband into focus and refused the suggestion adding, unwisely, that his leaving would cause her no discomfort; and returned to her tutor.

Her reaction was not well received. Making rude gestures to the room in general and to her in particular and walking backwards the while, he retired unsteadily and returned morosely to the hotel. His wife meanwhile, now unencumbered, enthusiastically continued to absorb Greek culture. Two hours and several ouzos later, she and her instructor left the scene and headed towards Kardamena.

Doubtless en route he told her of his occupation as a vendor of electrical goods, perchance he spoke of his present prosperity. And perhaps on their arrival at the village it was on the pretext of demonstrating his latest stock and providing tangible evidence of Kardamena's improved economy that he invited her into the shop, but the narrators were unsure of these minutiae. But it was there, so I was advised, that she succumbed to his charm and aftershave and was promptly short-circuited across a Bendix.

It is said that confession is good for the soul and I am sure that is so. However, I could not help but think that on that occasion it would have been better for all concerned had the fallen one not returned to her waiting husband and made the teasing announcement, 'You'll never guess what *I've* been doing!' And then elaborated.

The news did not go down well. Saying, 'Well *really*,' or words to that effect and pausing only to drain his bottle of Duty Free, the cuckold leapt to his feet, remonstrated physically with his spouse, clambered into his clothes and did the stairs to the foyer in one. There, and apparently acting upon a whim, he seized the alarm clock, staggered across the square, momentarily swayed before the shop of his tormentor, and hurled it through the window. Roused from their sleep by the sound of breaking glass, heavy-eyed observers saw him stand admiringly but uncertainly before his handiwork and then watched him disappear erratically into the dawn and along the long road to Kos. 'Po! po! po!' they said, Po! po! po!'

Unbelievably the story had a happy ending, the only permanent casualty being the alarm clock which was returned to its astonished owner later the same day. Equally unbelievable was the saga itself and I was much exercised by it as I left Stelio's and walked once more past the scene of the drama. Such things, I thought, could only happen in Greece; but the tale was retold to me more than once before I left the village, and with varying degrees of embroidery.

In that particular the people of Kardamena had remained constant. Nor, as I discovered during the coming days, had the majority of them changed in attitude. True, a middle-aged barber had dyed his hair to improve his chances with migratory birds during the summer season, much to the disquiet of his clients whose locks were attacked by distinctly shaky scissors by the end of August – or so they told me, and the eyes of some shopkeepers had drachmae in their pupils instead of smiles from the heart. They were, as a cynical Greek said, 'no longer seeing visitors as people but as money'; but the Kardamena of 1980 was not the Kardamena I had known of even the year before.

Materially the place had prospered. Agreed, no longer could I buy 'doppio yohourti', the delicious home-made thick skinned yoghurt made with goat's milk and which in flavour and texture eclipsed the production belt variety currently imported by the village: Mama Adam, widowed mother of Kardamena's best dancer, no longer made the former. Nor did her son dance as he used to do when the 'kephi', the spirit, moved him; fatter than he was, he was too busy with the auto-cycle hirings and the renting of rooms in his new house. And the cafeneons, the places where unshaven, corduroyed old men were wont to sit and while the hours away, as such were non-existent. Their tables were required for urgent use and strip-lighting and piped music had driven them away during the tourist months; but the little harbour on which they used to look through rheumy eyes had been improved and dredged.

Tavernas had sprung up along the shore. Patio furniture had arrived, white and brash and plastic-covered. So had the wide-screen coloured telly. Popcorn was being sold on the front. There were more tractors in the fields around the village and fewer oxen drawing wooden ploughs. In streets cleaner than they used to be there was a rash of trash and trinket shops, storeys were being added to existing houses, others were being built; and in kitchens house-wives stood admiringly before new washing machines and cookers. Kardamena had arrived. As Mr Macmillan would have said, 'they had never had it so good'. But Kardamena was no longer a fishing village.

It was a thriving tourist resort. The Big Operators had moved in. They had splattered the sea with pedalos, planted beach umbrellas in the sand and stuck up their posters and hoardings. 'Helio Tours Welcomes You' they proclaimed on the approach to the village; and so did Greko Trips and Troyways. And with their presence I sensed that the soul of Kardamena was guttering like a spent candle.

It had extended and was still extending, in all directions. Where once my feet had scuffed white dust I walked on concrete and past new dwellings with 'rooms to rent' signs. Near the western beaches a vast hotel had been completed. It had a night club and a swimming pool. And in the village itself and on the space where two Easters past the almirithra trees had grown in clumps and borne the hanging carcasses of sheep and goats freshly slaughtered for the Paschal feast, there was an eighty-roomed hotel.

When first I saw it I gazed in disbelief hoping perhaps that it was a mirage, but it was solid enough in its new vulgarity. Then, as I drank in this horror and looked further to its right, I saw something else which caused my pupils to constrict.

Close by, there was a small oblong building which after a good deal of difficulty I recognized as one in which the year before divers animals including a donkey, some piglets and a green and pink chicken like a neopolitan ice-cream on stilts, were housed for the night. It was a dry land Noah's Ark supervised by a Mrs Noah in the shape of a

bent old body who used to shout 'Cree! Cree! Cree!' to
the chickens, obscenities at the donkey and then fall down.
Of her there was no sign because, as I discovered later, she
was saying 'Cree! Cree! Cree!' and doling out mash in a
better place. What I did see, on the wall of the
establishment and written in psychedelic lettering and
colours, possibly in memory of the green and pink
chicken, was the word – PUB. Below it, and presumably
in case the first message had failed, was another: BAR.

Prurient curiosity more than thirst took me through its
doors that evening: it was quite a revelation. Mucked out
and furnished throughout in pine, the room had rush
matting upon the floor, low hessian-covered seats in the
corners and a long wooden bar from behind which a pale-
faced bemused little boy was serving beer in rough pottery
mugs. I ordered some, took a sip; and wished I had not
done so.

'Ti ine?' I said to the small boy, 'what is it?'
'Thenexero,' he said, shrugging his shoulders, 'I don't
know.' Nor did I but privately I entertained the thought
that there was a strong association between the brewer and
the former incumbents of the stable.

I pushed the mug towards him. 'Thenbarazi,' I said, 'it
doesn't matter – I'll have a cognac.' And turned my
attention to the present inmates. As far as I could see,
which was not easy because of the dim lighting, the room
appeared to be occupied mainly by voracious British girls
mostly dressed in slinky black skirts slashed to the thigh
and all doing their best to eat Greek – not moussaka, but
men; and to judge by the expressions on some of the faces
dyspepsia was rampant. Not, however, with all.

Close to me and preventing the bar from falling over
and clearly feeling little pain was an undesirable girl

She would shout 'Cree! Cree! Cree!' to the chickens, obscenities at the donkey and then fall down.

dressed in green lurex. That she had been in residence for some time was obvious. Equally it was patent that despite a deal of very hard work she had not been a social success.

'Excuse me,' she said in a strong Belfast brogue made even thicker by her night's activity, 'do you speak English? You do? So do I but,' she said swaying in the direction of an apprehensive tourist policeman and suppressing a burp with exaggerated gentility, 'he doesn't. At least he *says* he doesn't – I can't get through to him at all. I mean you'd think he'd understand sign language, wouldn't youse?' 'Well yes,' I said, thinking that even a retarded chimp would have found it difficult to mistake her semaphore, 'Yes I would, but perhaps,' I suggested as kindly as I could, 'perhaps he's on duty.'

She looked down upon my untouched glass of cognac. 'Oh, well,' she said. Then, with the air of one scraping the bottom of the barrel: 'Are you doing anything special yourself?' And drained the glass.

'Yes,' I said, 'yes, I am. I'm leaving.' And I went.

I stood for a moment under the stars taking in the good fresh air. From the airport at Antimachia beyond the silhouette of flat-topped hills the noise from a landing jet carried on the wind, the roar increasing as the pilot opened throttles and reversed thrust. I glanced at my watch and saw that it was past eight o'clock. Not long, I thought, before another excursion would arrive in the village. Also I began to think of food and of Kosta's brother Michaeli who had a taverna in the main street, 'Tried and True' I had dubbed it years ago and I began to walk towards it.

I was level with the new hotel when I was hailed. 'Yasu Yanni!' cried a voice from the shadows before it, 'Yasu Yanni mu!' it repeated and a large tent-shaped black form emerged and arms like legs of mutton went around my neck and pulled me to enormous bosoms. 'Chrissi!' I gasped as we came up for air. And we embraced again.

Chrissi was one of Kardamena's older and larger ladies, a widow whose husband had been drowned close to the shore area near Stelio's hotel just before I had first met her. Her grief then was almost as fresh as Poppi's present pain and she would kiss no man. At that time she was working in Stelio's kitchen and continued to do so until he closed the restaurant.

In a torrent of words she told me of her fortunes. 'Yanni,' she said, pointing excitedly to the hotel, 'do you know where I am working now, do you know?' She did not wait for an answer. 'It is there, Yanni, there in the big hotel! Ne Yanni, the *big* hotel! Ine poli orea Yanni – it is very beautiful! And Yanni,' she babbled, grasping my forearm and shaking it, 'do you know who is working there too? Phillipos! Phillipos with the beautiful face! Ne Yanni, Phillipos who waited at tables at Stelio's, it is there that he works with the cocktails! Go and see him Yanni, go and see him – he knows you are here. And now quickly I must go. Kalinichta Yanni mu, Yasas! Yasas!' And as suddenly as it had begun the verbal deluge ceased and off she went, bustling through the darkness like a great black bat.

I remembered Phillipos well. So did many women. Slim and elegant with finely moulded features and dreamy dark eyes, he reminded me of the Charioteer at Delphi. It would be interesting, I thought, to see the havoc he was creating on new territory.

I walked over the unmade ground to the entrance of the hotel, pushed open the double glass doors and entered a large reception lounge. It was, as Chrissi had said in her whirlwind account, very plush; and the quality of the piped music was excellent. However, had it been left to me I would not have chosen Cavalleria Rusticana as the piece most likely to evoke the ethos of Greece.

Considering the lateness of the season the hotel was well patronized. All the stools at the long bar were occupied. Behind it, bow-tied, white-shirted and fully occupied with a cocktail shaker, was Phillipos. He saw me, beamed in recognition and shook it in my direction.

'Yasu,' I called, and went to the far end of the bar and shook hands with him to the right of two girls. Both were in their twenties, both were wearing cheesecloth and neither took their eyes off him.

'Ti thapuis, Yanni,' he asked, 'What will you drink?'

'Epharisto,' I said, 'ouzo parakalo.'

The girl nearer to me noisily drew the last of her banana dacquiri through the straw. 'And can I,' she asked sucking it and still gazing at Phillipos, 'have another one?' There was a gurgle as her peeling blonde companion followed suit. 'And me,' she said huskily, 'piña colada.' 'But of course,' said Phillipos in English, 'Why not.'

Their eyes followed him as he prepared the drinks; and stayed on him when he set them down. 'On my house,' he said. And fluttered his lashes.

'Isighia!' I said, raising my glass – 'cheers!' And glanced around. 'There is plenty of work here?' He nodded. 'Ne. I am very busy. And,' he added softly and lowering his eyes, 'I think that later I shall be even more busy.' 'Yes,' I said looking at the mesmerized and freshly sucking girls, 'I think you will be.'

They were still watching him as he glided to the other end of the bar.

I took my drink, walked across the room and sat down close to a tired-looking representative of a travel firm seated behind a coffee table. Upon it was a glass of ouzo and a sign bearing her name. She was, as they say, doing her stint with her clients. It was complaint and information time. Towering over her was a large woman demanding to know why her sheets were not changed daily.

The representative was splendid in adversity. She would look into the matter she said and meanwhile could not express sufficient sorrow. She did not inquire, as I would have done: 'Do tell me – do you change *your* bed linen daily in Worplesdon? And if so and much more to the point, *why*?' Which is why I would be a total disaster as a travel rep and why they are complete wrecks at the end of a season.

I looked towards her sympathetically and she smiled wearily, acknowledging the aura. 'That's nothing,' she said, 'earlier I had one complaining that a cock crowed under her window each morning. What would she have me do – tell Manoli to have it stuffed?' And we laughed.

She took a sip of her ouzo and looked quizzically at me across the glass. 'I heard you speaking with Phillipos just now. Your Greek is very good. Almost as good as mine.' And we laughed again. 'You've been here many times, I believe?' I nodded. 'I've watched the place grow up. But I think you know Greece the better.'

'Maybe,' she said, 'perhaps; but I wish I'd seen Kardamena in its early days. But there,' and she shrugged her shoulders resignedly, 'that's the travel business for you. Greece is being Benidormed, isn't it? Which reminds me,' she said finishing her ouzo, 'I've another crowd coming in soon. They landed forty minutes ago – the last of the end-of-season cheap excursions. They're the worst, you know. They've been told the weather's uncertain now but they'll still blame me if it rains or the wind blows sand in their eyes. And if the women don't get a man within the first three days, whose fault will it be? Mine!'

She got up, straightened her skirt and picked up her name plate. 'Kalinichta,' she said holding out her hand, 'it's been nice meeting you.'

I stood up and watched her go. She was very attractive.

As she moved towards the exit two middle-aged men with glasses in their hands crossed from the bar and advanced towards our vacated seats, talking as they came. One was pink, large and very fat and gave the impression that he had only just been inflated. The other, similarly coloured, was very small. Their colouring told me they were recent arrivals; and their accents betrayed their origin. There is no mistaking the Bradford voice.

'By gow,' rumbled the fat one as they approached slowly in tandem like a music-hall act, 'I've supped some stuff in my time but bloody 'ell, I've 'ad nawt like this ouzo.' 'Yes I know,' said his companion in a shrill reedy voice, 'yes, it's unusual in't it? Um, yes. Like the food we 'ad yesterday. I mean –'

'The trouble with Greek food,' interrupted the Elephant and bringing them to a halt, 'is that it's all bloody spices and 'erbs.' 'Yes, I know it is,' said Tiny Wee, 'yes, yes I find it makes me –'

'It would,' said the Elephant interrupting again, 'it does. Me cousin, the chemist one at Pudsey, he told me that. He warned me. He were at Mee-ko-nos last year. Took him a week on't kaolin to get his stomach right. Oh aye.' He paused to blow his nose stentoriously into a large handkerchief. 'But yer know what I've done?' Tiny Wee shook his head. 'Well I'll tell yer,' said the Elephant breathing heavily, 'I've brought out fourteen tins of baked beans – just in case. Any road, let's get sat down. I told

'I find it makes me –'
'It would . . . it does.'

Edith we'd be 'ere but she were still on't toilet when I left, poor lass. And they're funny things an' all aren't they, toilets? Have you noticed how. . .'

It was a fascinating conversation and one to which I was loath to stop listening. Like the story of the hole in the window it proved yet again that fact is stranger than fiction. But, I wondered, why baked beans? Surely, I reasoned as I left for a meal and passed a pale lady who might have been the unhappy Edith on reprieve, baked beans were not the most sensible of iron rations. Moreover I think I was right. Three days later his face was still the same tone.

By the time I reached Michaeli's taverna in the main street it was well after nine o'clock but the place was still crowded. I had met Michaeli early that morning as I left Kosta's pension on my way to see Poppi but I had yet to be reunited with Oolah, his wife.

In her early fifties, Oolah was large, fat-splattered, swarthy and warty; and I adored her. Most of her day was spent bending over sizzling pans on the stove in her kitchen and it was over them that we embraced to the sound of frying chips and amid a general hubbub of welcome from other members of the family. It was a moving moment in which all joined, including Michaeli's mother-in-law and cousin and some time before the osculation stopped and the pop-eyed diners readdressed themselves to their meals.

Flanked by Oolah on one side and her sister on the other and with my arms around them both, I peered into the saucepans, chose bean soup, marides and salad, helped myself to a bottle and a glass and carried them to a small table next to the scullery door. Michaeli's son Yiorgo followed close on my heels.

Urgently he cleared the table of dirty plates and the remains of stuffed tomatoes, hurled them into the scullery sink and returned to wipe the table top and remove a chip from the chair. 'Epharisto,' I said and sat down with my glass and bottle. 'Parakalo,' said Yiorgo taking off its metal cap; and rushed back to the kitchen. Seconds later he reappeared with a pottery mug and banged it down on the table. It contained a plastic handled knife with a serrated blade, a bent fork and a discoloured soup spoon. Minutes afterwards and true to tradition my soup, whitebait, bread and salad all arrived together attended by a plastic lemon and the gift of another bottle. 'Kali orexi,' said Yiorgo. And wiped his nose on his sleeve.

Suddenly I felt at home. Michaeli at least had made no concessions to the Kardamena of the 'eighties. Nor had he altered. He was still as unpolished as his cutlery and his voice was as hoarse as ever it was. And he still wore tinted glasses as he did in the days when the taverna was noisy with Greek music from a juke box and filled with soldiers from the local garrison singing over their bottles. But his clientele had changed and the noise was a different kind.

The voices now were predominantly English with an admixture of German and Dutch. They rose and fell as I finished my soup, puncturing the air with cries of, 'I'm sticking to chicken, safe don't you think?' or 'Meatballs for me, you know what's in *them*,' and other wildly inaccurate statements. Nothing in this life is more uncertain than a Greek meatball. Perhaps, I pondered, it was a meatball that had laid the ailing Edith low; but with the conversation in the New Hotel fresh in my mind the utterances convinced me that the majority of English entertain an almost paranoid mistrust of Grecian food.

Gradually the noise level dropped as the visitors left,

some to go to the disco and others to take a last walk along the jetty before bed. By half past ten only one couple remained. Lugubrious and plum-coloured and occupying the table where so often I had sat with Vasili, they were eating spaghetti; with a knife. Eventually they too departed and the clearing up began. Pans were cleaned, tables wiped and I gave a hand in the kitchen. Then, with the long day's work nearly at an end we all sat down around a table and talked of the past and the present and future.

Ineludibly Vasili's name was mentioned and inevitably my eyes started to swim. Michaeli looked at me from behind his dark glasses. 'Oche!' he rasped, 'no tears. He would not want that. And do not forget, Yanni, he is very happy. He has no troubles, he has all the retsina he wants, and Yanni – it is all free! And in any case Yanni,' he said echoing the sentiments of Dimitri, 'ine e zoi – it is life!'

Michaeli was right. And wise. I thought of his words that night when I left his family close to midnight and stood alone on Kosta's roof looking seaward to the twinkling lights on the isles of Niceros and Yelli, and watched the moon sink lower. I remembered them when I walked the hills in the next few days, and I carried them with me when I made my goodbyes to Poppi and sailed at dawn for Rhodes from where I had come.

Michaeli was right. It is never sensible to look back and one cannot prevent change. Vasili's death had saddened me and so had the passing of the Kardamena I had known, but it was futile to mourn for either. They had gone and with them a way of village life; but the next generation of Kardameans will have no such memories and therefore no regrets. Nor, I reminded myself as I watched Kos grow smaller under the strengthening sun, will the tourists of the future. They will paddle their pedalos in their thousands or sit in the shade of beach umbrellas and hire out mopeds by the hundred. And the tills in the village will clink away and the men and the women and children will prosper; and that will be good. But, I thought, no matter how it changes, whenever I revisit it I shall always walk with ghosts.

That evening in Rhodes town I sat over an ouzo with a one-eyed Greek named George. He and his Swedish wife were old friends of mine and it was from their apartments that I had left for Kardamena.

George may have had only one eye through which he viewed the world with some realism and much cynicism, but he had a complete command of several languages, a splendid dry sense of humour, and a catholicity of interests of which one was tourism. He possessed also an asthmatic cat with a weak stomach which could, and did, present problems from time to time, and a sex-mad white mongrel called Bobaki. All in all it was an interesting household.

George listened carefully and with little interruption to the account of my visit.

'My dear Yanni,' he said offering me some pistachio nuts, 'you have a number of virtues but two great shortcomings. You are selfish and possessive. You treat Greece as a jealous lover does a beautiful mistress! You love her, extol her beauty and then become angry when others pay her attention! Yes Yanni,' he said, stifling my objection and wagging a finger, 'you want her all to yourself! No one else must come near her, no one else may touch her! And,' he continued, 'she must always be just as she was when you first met her – her face must never change! Is that not true my friend? Admit it!'

I grinned into my glass. 'I like the analogy,' I said, 'but to be fair, Yiorgo mu, it's not the change of face I dislike – it's the way the make-up has been applied.'

George threw back his head and laughed. 'Yanni,' he said, continuing to analogize, 'a growing girl is conscious of her potentials. She tries hard to attract. And the more men she can please the better she likes it; but she gets herself screwed en route! And that,' he said, earthily bringing the parallel to an end and finishing his drink, 'is what has happened to Greece – she has lost her innocence. Tourism is a big part of our economy now. And Yanni, what you have seen in Kardamena is taking place throughout the Islands. It is even happening to Karpathos!'

'In *Karpathos*?' I echoed incredulously.

'In Karpathos!' repeated George slapping his knee and frightening the cat, 'even in Karpathos.' He chuckled and got up to replenish our ouzos. 'Do you remember when you first went there? When I joined you in Pigadia?'

'I do,' I said, 'vividly.' George handed me my glass. 'And Mama Barbunia?' he asked.

'Especially Mama Barbunia,' I said, 'what a woman!'
'What a doll!' cried George, 'What a cukla! Here's to her – Viva Barbunia!' And choked on his drink. He was still spluttering when he took off his spectacles and wiped his good eye.

'You know, Yanni,' he said, replacing them and straightening his face, 'you really should go and see her again! Two years is a long time to keep a girl waiting! There she is, unrequited and –'

He broke off to stare at a spot near my chair. 'That bloody cat,' he said through his teeth. And made for the door.

'Serve you right,' I said. And laughed unkindly. 'And who knows,' I called after him, 'perhaps I shall go!'

And I did. But it was my first visit to Karpathos I remembered better. And it was on George's recommendation that I went there.

CHAPTER II

Cats, Canaries and Catastrophes

I T WAS IN THE late Spring of 1978 when I wrote to George seeking his advice. I had just returned from my third consecutive visit to Kardamena where I had taken part in the Greek Easter festivities and greatly though I was tempted to return in the Autumn I felt that I should spread my wings and explore more of the Dodecanese. Had he, I asked, any suggestions?

With customary Greek urgency he replied in the August.

Had I, he inquired, considered Karpathos? If not, I should do so. As yet it was not 'touriste' and he thought I might like it. The island, he wrote, was halfway between Kos and Crete, comparatively small and very beautiful. Anyway, he suggested, why should I not come to Rhodes in September and stay with them for a few days? Then we could discuss the matter fully and if I decided to go on to Karpathos nothing could be simpler. It was only forty minutes' flying time from Rhodes and accommodation there would be no problem as he had friends who owned a pension. Perhaps I would let him know. . .

I did so. By return. And on Wednesday, 20th September 1978 I flew to Rhodes from Gatwick.

The flight was relatively uneventful and only made memorable for me by an elderly lady who announced at regular intervals to all and sundry that this was her first flight and that she was a little nervous. As she put it rhetorically, 'one never knows what's going to happen, does one!' 'No,' we answered affording her scant comfort, 'one doesn't, does one?' And promptly re-read the notes on emergency drill. She was an able disturber of one's peace of mind. My most poignant memory of the lady was of her standing in the lavatory queue in the front of the aeroplane and reading a paperback entitled *Tales of the Unexpected*. Thus engrossed, and so bewitched was she by the imagination of Roald Dahl that when her turn came she chose the wrong door; and went into the pantry. Backing from that with an 'Oh–dear-me' and a 'ha-ha-ha' she was next seen being escorted from the flight-deck. However, none the worse for the experience she was met at the airport by a female cousin to whom forthwith she related her adventures, and I was greeted by George with a waiting taxi.

It was seven o'clock by the time we reached George's apartments, and the heat of the day was leaving Rhodes. There we were given an effusive welcome by his Swedish wife Anna-Marie and his aged mother, Bobaki and another dog of equally dubious parentage named Picolo; and five cats. Both George and Anna-Marie were susceptible to waifs and strays and the cat and dog population in the ménage was always uncertain. So, too, were the animals' habits.

Refreshed by a plate of peaches and some grapes but tired and sticky after the journey, I took a shower, removed a black tom with a much chewed ear from its place on my bed and lay down to watch the light fade slowly beyond the open balcony windows. Gently my eyes closed.

I did not hear my door open but I did feel Bobaki's wet nose in my ear as he blew me into consciousness. 'The sleep of the Just,' said George softly from the doorway and moving into the room to switch on a table lamp, 'bettered only by the sleep of the just after. Ne, Bobaki?' He bent down and patted the dog who leered and lolled its tongue in dumb appreciation of the well-worn sally. 'And at half-past eight,' said George addressing me, 'it is time for a drink, I think. So, when you are ready, Yanni, come through. We shall be in the lounge. 'Ella, Bobaki!' He paused at the door. 'Oh by the way,' he said as the animal scampered past him, 'I would not let Bobaki kiss you like that if I was you. I know where his nose has been. . .'

I lay still for a moment, staring at the ceiling and digesting this latest news and wishing I had less imagination. Then, swinging my legs over the side of the bed, I prepared to make myself presentable, paying particular attention to my left ear. Fifteen minutes later, shaved and dressed in a short-sleeve shirt and slacks, I joined them in the sitting-room.

'Ah,' said George gesturing to Anna-Marie and Aged Mum as I entered, 'kissed by Prince Bobaki, the Sleeping Beauty returns to life! Ella, Yanni – sit down.' I did. On a cat.

'Thenbarazi,' said George, unmoved as it exhaled violently beneath my buttocks and screeched across the room pursued by Bobaki, 'it does not matter.' He handed me a drink. 'Stinyamas!' he said, 'here's to us!' 'Skäl!' said Anna-Marie ever faithful to her country despite her matrimonial alliance with the Greeks; and we raised our glasses to one another.

'Now,' said George, 'to business. Karpathos!'

'Ah yes,' I said, sinking back expectantly into my armchair, 'Karpathos. Tell me all about it.'

'I cannot tell you *all* about it,' said George taking a sip at his ouzo, 'because I do not know it so well, but in fact we are going there ourselves on Saturday for three, perhaps four, days. And Yanni,' he said, winking at me, 'it would be fun if you were there as well. Ne, Anna-Marie?' He looked across to his wife who was sitting next to Aged Mum and nursing a moth-eaten tortoiseshell.

'Yars! Yars!' she said, beaming at me, 'we would have der larf-er Yanni! Elways der larf-er when you play der feul-er! And also Yanni,' she continued, emotionally clasping her left bosom and shutting her big blue eyes, 'it is so, so so bew-ti-ful this island! Yars! So feul of der nai-cha – eulways der nai-cha. Aah!' She sighed in ecstasy and opened her eyes again. 'Yu laiker nai-cha Yanni? Der-trees-and-der-leefs-and-der-flowers-and-der-so-on?'

'Yes,' I said, and trying hard not to fall into her rhythm, 'I like them very much.'

She beamed again. 'And also Yanni,' she went on, holding the brown and yellow unfortunate under its fore paws and rubbing noses with it as hunchbacked and stiff-legged it dangled before her, 'there are der ani-ma-les! Many many ani-ma-les! Yu laiker ani-ma-les, Yanni? Yars? Der poo-sy car-ters?' She sounded dubious

'Of course I do,' I said reassuringly and avoiding the gaze of the one I had flattened and which was eyeing me with something akin to loathing from under a chair, 'I'm very fond of them. Indeed,' I said, 'sometimes I like them more than people!'

'Especially tourist people,' said George dryly and breaking up what was promising to evolve into a nature appreciation class. 'Ne, Yanni?'

'Oche!' I said, raising my hand in protest, 'be fair! Some tourists.'

'*All* tourists,' said George uncompromisingly and brushing my objections aside, 'but no matter. In Karpathos they will not cast their shadows on your circles! Karpathos does not cater for the hordes. Nor does the older generation want them. Or need them. Oche! There is plenty of money in Karpathos, plenty.'

For the next fifteen minutes I listened to him attentively and without interruption. Karpathos, I learned, is a rich island where most families enjoy a high standard of living. Regularly they are in receipt of money sent to them by expatriates working in the coal mines or the car industry in America. And, George assured me, wagging his index finger, the amounts are not chicken-feed. One has only to look at the style of the houses, new and old, in the hill villages of Aperi and Othos and Menetes to see palpable evidence of the wealth. Then of course, he continued, there are the Karpathians who have returned to the island to retire and who draw United States pensions. They are very comfortably off. 'And good luck to them too,' said George bringing the appreciation to a close, 'God knows they have had to work hard and long enough for their rewards.'

'And the people themselves,' I asked, 'what are they like?'

George carefully selected an olive from an alabaster dish. 'Well,' he said, chewing it thoughtfully, 'the natives are not exactly hostile, but I think you will find them a little less light-hearted than other islanders. In a word,

Yanni,' he said, expelling the olive-stone into his cupped hand and putting it in the dish, 'they are – katsufis.'

'Katsufis,' I repeated, puzzled. 'Solemn,' said George, 'or if you prefer it,' he elaborated, airing his command of colloquial English, 'po-faced.'

'Tru, tru,' said Anna-Marie re-entering the conversation and sounding like a tweeter telephone, 'tru, tru – they do not larf teu much-er, but they are so so nice, the pee-pals. And Yanni,' she continued, preparing to go into another trance, 'eulways there is der nai-cha, eulways der –'

'I can't wait to see it!' I said, and crossed the room to embrace her through a haze of cat fur. 'Bravo!' said George rising to his feet, 'When do you want to go? Tomorrow?' I nodded. 'Why not,' I said, 'if it's possible?' 'Nothing,' said George making for the door, 'is impossible in Greece if you have friends and a telephone!'

Minutes later he reappeared. 'Endaxi!' he said, clapping his hands and rubbing them together, 'with two phone calls all is arranged! The Papadakises, the friends we shall be with on Saturday, say they will be pleased to put up with you for quite a few days, so that is good.' 'That is kind of them,' I said, ignoring one of George's rare excursions into inaccurate syntax, 'thank you very much.' 'Not a bit,' said George, 'I am sure they mean it. And they will meet you off the bus in Pigadia tomorrow morning. They are nice people, Yanni. Katsufis but nice.'

'And my air ticket?' I asked. 'That,' said George patting his stomach, 'we can collect on our way to town. And now let's go – my ulcer is in need of feeding!' He grimaced and reached into his shirt pocket. 'Po! po! po!' he said, and unwrapped an antacid tablet. Like most Greeks George was much concerned about his health. Indeed, no Greeks worth their salt will admit to being wholly free of some ailment, real or imaginary, and conversation on the topic is to them what the weather is to the British.

'Yars, yars,' said Anna-Marie, ridding herself of the tortoiseshell and brushing her skirt vigorously, 'eulways der ulcer. Sure, sure we go.' She patted George affectionately on the cheek. 'Androoli mu,' she said, 'my little husband'; and disappeared into the bedroom followed by three cats. Aged Mum, attended by Bobaki and Picolo, moved into another room to watch television. When we left she was glued to the screen watching a football match and liberally feeding herself and the dogs on sweetmeats. Aged Mum was hooked on football. And sticky things. So too, it seemed, were Bobaki and Picolo. 'I hope,' said George on our way past them, 'that she does not overdo it with the baclava. Their stomachs are not so strong.'

The taverna in which we ate was inside the walls of the old town, close to St Catherine's Gate. Unremarkable in appearance and decorated inside with pseudo-ancient wall-plates, crabshells and crayfish tails, and three hanging cages of singing birds and finches, it offered some of the best food to be had in Rhodes town. The proprietor, Christos, was a solid middle-aged, moustached, kind man whose thinning grey hair topped a pale tragi-comic face in which honest red-rimmed grey eyes quickly could cloud or sparkle as his mood dictated. That night they were lively and warm with affection as he greeted us and embraced me wholeheartedly. It had been a year since we had first met and become friends and his welcome was as emotional as his farewell had been when we had said goodbye.

Swiftly the ouzo appeared, tall thick glasses clinked together in salutation, meze was ordered, and soon the blue and white plastic tablecloth was covered with pyrex dishes. Brown, humbug-coloured little snails in tomato and garlic sauce, warm pink butterbeans in oil, fried aubergines, tarama and houmus, tsatsiki and salad – all to be followed by squid cooked in wine, sweet red mullet and bottles of retsina. 'Kali orexi!' called Christos from the kitchen as we sucked out the snails like hungry thrushes, 'yasas!' we answered him as we sipped and mopped up the sauces with the bread and addressed ourselves to the fishes, 'ine kalo! Poli kalo!'

It was a magnificent meal and one to which we did full justice. Nothing was wasted. Fish-heads and carcasses for the socially deprived and ever hungry cats were scooped into a bag, and we rounded off with huge platefuls of sliced red water melon and cold green grapes. In the background a cassette played bouzoukoi music, outside on the verandah a small party of raucous Greeks burst into song and one of the canaries trilled in competition despite the lateness of the hour. It was a noisy happy atmosphere and one in which I relaxed completely.

George who had eaten sufficient to quieten a dozen ulcers lolled back in his chair. Replete and comfortable, his arms hanging limply by his sides and with fingers clicking rhythmically he began to join in the singing. So too did three unshaven seamen at a nearby table, and so did I while Christos and Anna-Marie clapped their hands in time.

It was a sprightly, bawdy little song dedicated to a girl named Maria in a yellow dress by a randy gentleman who apart from making his intentions plain made disparaging remarks about her husband. Vasili had taught it to me and I sang it with verve. 'Bravo!' shouted the unshaven ones as the song came to an end, and banged their hands on their table. 'Bravo! He knows the words! He can sing in Greek!

Poso lena – what's your name?' 'Yanni,' I said. 'Ah?' they chorused, 'Yanni! Baba Yanni!' And off they went into another song about a dirty old man with a donkey and an eye for the girls. It is as old as the hills of Greece and inevitably sung whenever the retsina flows and a Yanni is present. I had learned 'Baba Yanni' in Andros on my Name Day, and hungry for more applause, again I added my voice to theirs. Unfortunately I was denied the vocal triumph of my first contribution. Disturbed by an errant grape pip, halfway through the fourth verse and when my mouth was wide open, my dental plate fell out and landed in my lap.

As a show stopper I have yet to meet its equal. The applause was deafening. With streaming eyes and as one man the seamen requested an encore, George patted Anna-Marie on the back, Christos banged another bottle of retsina on the table and I was given another ovation as I replaced my teeth; but the act had been the ultimate in ice-breaking. Nothing quite like it, I was assured, had ever been seen in Rhodes and they were grateful to George for my presence. Where, he was asked in his capacity of impresario and as if I was no longer present, had he found me? How long had he known me? Where had I learned Greek? How long was I staying?

'Only tonight,' I interrupted, physically re-establishing myself, 'tomorrow I go to Karpathos.' The seaman called Spiros looked at me. 'Karpathos,' he rasped and airing his stilted English, 'What for you wan' go Karpathos?' 'Because,' I said, 'I am told it is very beautiful.' 'Yars, yars,' chimed Anna-Marie going into her routine and gazing at the canary, 'eulways der nai-cha! So, so bew-ti-ful.' 'Ne,' agreed Spiros grudgingly, 'but not too beautiful.' He leaned towards me. 'You know which hiland is the too beautiful? I tell you!' He tapped his chest aggressively. 'My hiland! Tilos! You go see Tilos, ne? Then if you not say Tilos is the too beautiful' – and here he broke off to screw his index finger into the side of his nose, 'na mu tripeesis ti meeti – you can put a hole through my nose!'

He looked around him, nodding in agreement with himself. 'Sosta?' he inquired of the company, 'true?' He was a very large man and more than a little drunk and although inter-island rivalry in the Dodecanese on principle called for debate, nobody seemed inclined to argue with him. 'Yar yar,' said Anne-Marie diplomatically and beaming at him, 'Tilos is so bew-ti-ful.' 'Bravo!' said Spiros, pleased that his island remained top of the league table but continuing to extol its virtues, 'also cheap. Not like Karpathos. There one lettuce – you know how much? Thirty drachs! Ne, ma to theo – I tell the truth! And the water,' he continued, surprising me by its mention for it seemed unlikely that he ever touched it, 'not nice. Make you go –' He frowned, searching for the English and capitulated. 'Parthee,' he said. I looked puzzled. 'Fart,' said George.

'Ne!' cried Spiros slapping the table, delighted by George's skill as an interpreter, 'sosta! Fart!' And pursing his lips he ensured that no one remained in ignorance of what he had had in mind.

His success as an artiste was almost as complete as mine had been and it was some moments before the laughter and hubbub died down. It was then that we became aware that the music had stopped and that the canary was no longer singing. And it was then that we noticed Christos.

He was standing in front of the cage, looking worried. George called over to him. 'What's the matter?' he asked. Christos made no reply. In silence we watched him

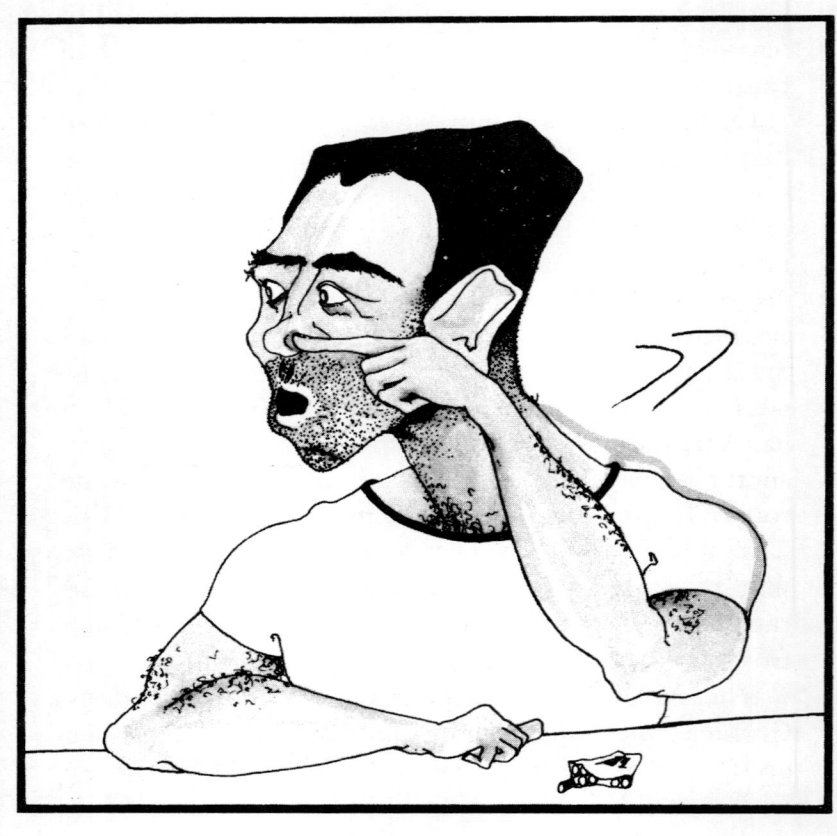

'You can put a hole through my nose.'

unhook the small wire door, open it, and carefully put his hand inside. Above it, two finches mutely hopped from perch to perch; and in silence we saw him withdraw his hand, re-fasten the latch and stand holding the dead canary. Anna-Marie gave a little gasp. 'Oh no!' she said.

Our chairs scraped on the terrazzo floor as we pushed them back and walked slowly over to Christos. He stood quite still, holding the little bird in his cupped hand and looking down at it with filling eyes. Uncomprehendingly he shook his head. 'But why?' he said, 'she was so happy just now.' He blew gently into the soft yellow down as if willing the bird back to life. Then, lifting it with his other hand, he held it against his stubbled cheek, and dampened the fluff with tears. His sad clown's face looked at me. 'I had her when she was a chick,' he said, and pointed to another cage. 'That is her mother over there.' Across the room the other canary unconcernedly preened its wing. Christos stared at it, then sighed and shrugged his shoulders. 'Ah well,' he said, 'that is life.' Roughly he rubbed the back of his hand across his eyes and turning from us, took the bird away.

It had been a poignant little scene. All of us had shared in Christos's distress and shortly afterwards we made our goodbyes and left, Spiros and his companions for their ship in the commercial port and the three of us to walk home through the old town.

It was past midnight when we left Christos, and at the end of the season few people walked the medieval streets of Rhodes. A young couple strolled towards us, arms entwined and totally engrossed. They stopped to kiss at the foot of the library steps and then moved on and passed us, still looking into each other's eyes. 'Ah yes,' said George, 'soon to bed for them, I think. And why not? At this time

Rhodes is made for lovers. Ne, Anna–Marie?' And squeezed her hand. For all his worldliness George was a romantic at heart.

We walked on. Through little squares with playing fountains, along ancient streets with neon signs, 'Tasty Restaurant' and 'Pub Dancing', past tailors' dummies in shop windows smiling waxily at flagstones trodden once by armoured soldiers, and down the long Street of the Knights. And there in the stillness I swore I could hear their horses' hooves and the clank of steel as they rode towards the castle. And I heard their voices murmuring in the shadows in the tongues of the Knights of St John. From Auvergne and Provence, Italy and France, from Germany, England and Spain. The street was full of their ghosts.

'My friend,' said George breaking my reverie, 'you have been away! Six hundred years I think. Am I correct?' I laughed. 'Quite right,' I said, 'you must be a thought reader!' 'Maybe,' said George, 'but I often make that journey myself in the quiet of the winter months. That's when the knights ride most.'

We left the ghosts behind us as we passed under the gateway leading us back to modern Rhodes, and cobbles gave way to tarmac when we crossed the bridge with its shuttered kiosks which spanned the dried-up castle moat. From it came the acrid smell of captive deer confined within it. George wrinkled his nose and sniffed. 'I like animals,' he said, 'but not when they are –'. He stopped in his tracks. 'Damn!' he said, 'the cats! I've forgotten the fish-heads!'

Anna-Marie looked aghast in the moonlight. 'Oh Yiorgo,' she wailed, 'you haven't?' She peered at him for confirmation, 'Yars,' she said as his disquiet was made apparent, 'yar, yar, you ha-ver! The li–tel bir–der, yar? It ma-der you forget-er?' 'Possibly,' said George, grasping at a welcome straw, 'yes, of course, the little bird.' We walked the rest of the way in silence.

Oddly there was no sign of the animals when we returned to the apartments. 'Kali nichta,' said George at my bedroom door. 'Sweet dreams,' said Anna-Marie, kissing me on both cheeks. 'Yes,' endorsed George, unbuttoning his shirt, 'and short ones. We have to be at the airport by nine-thirty.' They disappeared in the direction of the kitchen and I washed, pulled the sheet over me and prepared for sleep. Fifteen minutes later I was alerted by raised voices and a strong smell of disinfectant wafting under my door. I got out of bed, dressed in my underpants and unwisely went in search of an explanation.

Halfway to the kitchen I encountered Anna-Marie carrying a floor cloth, 'Ha-ha,' she said mirthlessly, attempting to wave its sodden weight in my direction, 'I am afraid that Bobaki and Picolo have, how you might say, been sick-er. Yars. It was the baclava, I think. Also,' she continued, like a character from an Ibsen play, 'the li-tel car-ters have made a small small mistake.' 'They have not made a small small mistake,' said George, appearing with another cloth, 'they have made a large mistake – on the bed. And if I were you Yanni,' he said, glowering with his one eye, 'I would get some sleep while you can. That is,' he added, looking at Bobaki who was eyeing him sheepishly from the doorway, '*if* you can . . .'

CHAPTER III

Solemnities and Stomach Rumbles

Breakfast that thursday morning was a sombre affair. Aged Mum, indirectly but clearly responsible in part for the mayhem of the previous night, was uncommunicative, the disgraced dogs were curled listlessly in their basket, and Anna-Marie had the appearance of a washed-out panda. However, she mustered a smile when George and I left by taxi for the airport, wished me a good journey and reminded me that the two of them would be sailing to Karpathos in the Saturday ferry. Anna-Marie did not enjoy flying.

George left me waiting in the departure lounge looking through the windows at the aircraft in which I was to fly. Named *Mykonos* and painted blue and white, it was a high-winged, twin-engined sixteen seater with rectangular boomed rudders decorated with the olympic emblem and was designed to be seaworthy if the occasion demanded. Seen from a distance this seemed to me to be a very prudent piece of engineering and a later and closer inspection did little to alter my initial appreciation. I could quite understand Anna-Marie's preference for ferries.

Shortly after George's departure the flight was announced and together with a quorum of Germans, eight assorted Greeks and three other English including a middle-aged lady named Gladys, I walked across the tarmac, watched the luggage being stowed in the rear of the aircraft and then jostled my way through the hatch-back.

An elderly Greek woman dressed in black and nursing an even more mature Greek cheese, cushioned herself next to me, adjusted her seat belt, and clutched her crucifix. A member of the crew of two recited the litany of the emergency drill in three languages and was listened to attentively by the Germans and ignored by the Greeks. The English talked throughout the recital. The narrator ended by wishing us all 'kalo taxithe' and dispensing multi-coloured boiled sweets for which Gladys said 'ta' and hoped that she wouldn't be sick. A hessian curtain was pulled across the pilot's compartment, the engines roared to full throttle, all the Greeks crossed themselves, and with a shudder the pregnant sparrow left the ground.

On we droned, across the blue Aegean, passing over toy fishing boats and ferries and nearer and nearer to Karpathos. Thirty five minutes later we saw its coastline and flew parallel to the island, down from the barren mountainous north, past steep and craggy woodsides in the middle and then towards a fertile plain in the south. Ahead of us lay a gravel landing strip. Steadily losing height we approached it erratically and with what appeared to me, as an ex-pilot, a cavalier disregard for one of the basic principles of flying, namely, to keep the aircraft steady. Steeply the wings dipped, first to starboard then to port, levelled, and then slowly returned to starboard. Next to me the parcel of cheese detached itself from its owner's lap, fell into the gangway and burst open.

The smell of vintage goat increased. At two hundred feet above the runway and as the port wing dipped again, I started to sweat profusely. Nor was my anxiety blunted by the sight of another small plane lying rusting and unloved on the side of the track. We skimmed past it and I closed my eyes as the ground came up to meet us. Two separate jarring bumps and the squeal of tyres in anguish told me that we had landed, albeit without the three wheels of the aircraft meeting the ground in unity. The propellers clattered into silence, the Greeks stopped crossing themselves and the pilot appeared smoking a cigarette and wearing an expression of great satisfaction. From the rear of the machine came the sound of Gladys in extremis.

We staggered out into fierce sunlight, and a warm wind blew dust into our eyes. It was very hot. To our right, a stubbled man dressed in shabby blue trousers and a collarless shirt, wheeled away a trolley containing a portable fire-extinguisher. Rejoicing in the title of fire-control officer he seemed disappointed, if not dejected, that he had not been required to use the contents of his syphon. He too was one of the world's smokers. Two other men similarly attired and addicted, shambled towards us pushing a luggage truck. Halfway to their destination, one was overcome with a paroxysm of coughing and was obliged to sit down on the vehicle to recover. With the cigarette still glued to his lower lip, he watched us through streaming eyes as we straggled towards the small concrete building known as the terminal.

The Greeks were greeted emotionally by friends and relations and on receipt of their luggage were bundled into waiting cars and driven away, cheeses and all, in clouds of dust. The remainder of us stood by our cases awaiting the return of the driver of an airport bus marked 'Pigadia' whence it had brought passengers bound for Rhodes in the same machine which we had vacated. I wished them joy.

Our departure for Pigadia was to be delayed by half an hour but the interval was not without incident. Still smoking a cigarette the fire officer shuffled back to the aeroplane dragging his appliance behind him and took up his station whilst the plane was refuelled; and a small table and two chairs were placed in the open. The latter was occupied by clerical workers of the airline and the former covered quickly by documents and papers most of which immediately blew away. The ensuing chase and recapture took place against a background of cheers from the spectators. The clerks, however, were not amused. They were, as George would have said, 'katsufis'. Meanwhile, the outgoing passengers, the majority of whom were British, were separated into their respective sexes by a policeman and asked politely to remain so divided. The reason for this soon became apparent.

To the left of the doorway of the building was a cubicle constructed of canvas and not dissimilar to a fortune teller's booth. Outside it and holding back the entrance flap stood a very butch unsmiling lady in overalls. Raising one finger she beckoned to the waiting crocodile of women. 'One only plis,' she boomed, and disappeared inside to be followed by the first candidate who emerged fifteen seconds later from the other side looking a little shaken and adjusting her bra.

Rapidly the others followed her and we watched fascinated as the hessian walls became agitated and gasps and giggles and an icy 'well really' came from within them. The last to reappear was a gaunt lady in her late fifties. 'Well Muriel,' she shrilled, addressing the previous incumbent in the cut glass accents of the better Home Counties, 'all I can say is that that's the first time I've had *that* done to me by a woman! Too droll!' Presumably when it came to the men's turn to be investigated the Medusa was replaced by a male counterpart but we were not to be enlightened for at that moment we were called to the bus and driven away.

With the sea on our right we climbed away from the plain and drove into gorse-covered craggy purple hills. Then, dropping down once more we followed the long, steep, winding road to Pigadia, ten miles away on the coast. Roadside shrines and little churches slipped by us as we motored on, and above us and on distant slopes, the sun reflected off the white sides and terracotta roofs of houses in hill villages. I resolved to visit them and tried to orientate myself and read their names on a map stuck up by the driver's seat, but the bus swayed too much for comfort. Abruptly the sea vanished as we took a corner and then as suddenly, reappeared ahead of us as we straightened out. And there it remained in view until at noon we saw it on our left as we approached the outskirts of the little town, honked our way slowly around the corners of its narrow streets and quayside, and came to a halt at the harbour's end. The driver switched off the engine and swivelled around in his seat. 'Welcome to Karpathos, folks,' he twanged, 'have a good day.' It was the first but not the last time I was to hear the sound of the Bronx on the island.

The door of the bus jack-knifed open and we stepped down into a street much busier than I had imagined it would be, but as I was to learn, Pigadia is the main part of the island and the place to which people from all over Karpathos come to shop and do business. A travel representative came across to meet the German and English parties and escorted them to a Japanese station-wagon. The former departed shouting at all within earshot and my fellow countrymen left telling Gladys she would feel better after a wash and they were sure it would come off with sponging. I watched them leave for their respective hotels and awaited my turn to be claimed. I did not wait long.

A stocky bespectacled man wearing black trousers and an open-necked shirt under many chins, detached himself from a nearby group of onlookers and advanced towards me with measured steps. I adjudged him to be in his early sixties. He halted before me and cleared his throat.

'Mr. Ebdon?' he inquired sombrely and in a manner similar to that employed by Stanley when meeting Livingstone, 'Mr John Ebdon?' I admitted to it. 'Andrei Papadakis,' he intoned, presenting invisible credentials, 'welcome to the island of Karpathos.'

Solemnly we shook hands. 'We have,' he said, continuing to speak in perfect English, 'heard much about you from our friend Mr George Zagorianos. Yes, a very great deal.' 'Ah well,' I said lightly, wondering what George had disclosed, 'you mustn't believe it all, you know!' And gave a carefree laugh. The pleasantry sank without trace.

'Mr Zagorianos,' pursued my host to be, 'is an old friend. We have,' he said heavily, 'known each other for thirty years.' He paused to allow me to digest the time scale. 'And now, Mr Ebdon, if you will come with me? The pension is not far from here. . .'

Obediently and subdued by the unaccustomed formality, I picked up my bag and we moved ponderously up the street. Already I had begun to appreciate the accuracy of George's character assessment of the locals. If Papadakis was anything to go by plainly they did not readily fling their caps in the air and dance naked in the light of the moon.

We walked for some three hundred yards along the front and then stopped before a general purpose store. It had a double-fronted window, one part of which was given to a montage of posters advertising ferry trips and excursions and the other to a haphazard display of television sets and pyrex tableware. 'My son's,' said Papadakis pointing to the posters. And shook his head. 'The young will turn Karpathos into a Mykonos unless they have a care.' His jowls quivered with misgiving.

The rooms of Papadakis's pension were above the shop. 'Please,' he said, standing at the doorway of a flight of marbled steps which led to them, 'follow me.' He mounted them, breathing heavily. At the top the stairway curved left and we entered a small hall and thence into a passageway which ran the length of the building to balconies at either end. The one to the left of us faced seaward, the other, as I was to discover later, an overgrown area mainly occupied by cats. Happily we turned left.

'Allow me,' said Papadakis opening the door of one of the three adjoining bedrooms on his right, and stepped back to allow me to enter. It was a pleasant room. Simply, but comfortably furnished, it contained two beds one of which was positioned under the window opening on to the communal balcony, a wash basin and a hanging cupboard. The walls were painted pale blue and decorated with framed coloured photographs of Karpathos and the floor, like all the others in the building, was terrazzo.

I put down my suitcase, crossed to the window and

looked out. The view was magnificent. 'I hope,' said Papadakis who had followed me in, 'that you will be comfortable here? It is,' he pronounced, 'one of the best two rooms in the house. The other,' he said reverently, 'will be for the use of Mr and Mrs Zagorianos when they arrive. That, too, has a view.' 'And is that occupied now?' I asked conversationally. He nodded. 'Yes,' he said sombrely, 'it is. By a young, Single Woman.'

He paused and pursed his lips. 'I am not,' he advanced, and as if addressing a meeting of the City Fathers, 'always happy about having Single Women to stay. They can, Mr Ebdon, bring problems.' He came closer to me and his voice dropped a semi-tone. 'You know what I mean,' he said. 'However,' he continued pontifically, and dashing any hopes I might have entertained, 'I am pleased to say that this one is very Proper. And now let me show you the toilet.' 'Please do,' I said, grateful that he had anticipated my question; and followed him through the door and obliquely across the passage.

Papadakis tried the handle. 'Oriste,' said a voice from within. 'Oh,' said Papadakis, 'sighnomi – I beg your pardon.' 'Tipota,' said the voice – 'don't mention it.'

'That,' said Papadakis, speaking of the occupant as if he was absent, 'is Mr Manoli, another of our gentleman guests.' He frowned. 'He is not usually in at this time.' Obviously disturbed by Mr Manoli's break with routine, my guide led the way down the passage and pushed open the door of another cubicle. 'As you can see,' he said, 'there is also a shower. Unfortunately I cannot show you how it works for at the moment there is not water anywhere in the town.' 'Oh dear,' I said. And thought of Gladys.

'Yes,' said Papadakis mournfully, 'water is one of our problems. And another,' he added even more lugubriously, 'is the plumbing.' He looked hard at the lavatory and then at me. 'It is most important,' he pounded, 'not to put papers in the toilet, but in the bin.' He indicated the ancillary equipment and cleared his throat. 'I cannot tell you, Mr Ebdon,' he tolled, 'the trouble we have when papers are put down the toilet;' and then proceeded to elaborate. At length. I half listened to the case histories and thought how well he would recite Dylan Thomas. . .

Eventually the list of transgressions came to an end and we moved from the scene of the crimes and back to the hall. Papadakis looked at his watch. 'No doubt,' he inquired, 'you will be going for a meal? It is now one o'clock.' 'No,' I said, 'I seldom eat much in the middle of the day. Usually just fruit.' 'Then perhaps,' he said gravely, 'I may send you up some grapes? The shops will be shutting until late afternoon.' 'How kind of you,' I said. 'Not at all,' he intoned, and inclined his head. 'Goodbye for the present, Mr Ebdon. I hope you enjoy your day.' 'I'm sure I shall,' I said, 'particularly when the water returns.' 'Ah yes,' he said, 'the water. I will send you a pail with the grapes.' And bowing again, he took his leave of me.

I watched him go, wondering if he would ever call me by my christian name and what might happen if I suggested that he did so. Possibly a coronary, I thought; but humourless and stuffy though he was, undoubtedly he was a kind man. And as good as his word; both water and grapes arrived within minutes. They were brought by his wife with her hair in curlers. She too did not appear to be the jolliest of souls.

I made my ablutions and went on to the balcony to take stock of my surroundings. I liked what I saw. I looked out over the deep blue waters of a semi-circular bay skirted on the left by long sandy beaches. Silver-grey and olive knolls rose from the shore, growing into steeply rising purple hills. Higher and higher they climbed, ridge upon ridge and beyond them, smoky in the heat haze of the early afternoon, ranged distant mountains with grey-fringed fleecy clouds hovering near their peaks. On my right, fishing boats bobbed at anchor below a little quay; and beyond, half hidden by houses the walled arm of the main anchorage reached further into the bay. Below me on the railed sea front, shirt-sleeved and bracered anglers cast long lines over a narrow stretch of dirty sand, rested their rods across the bars, and then sat down on slatted benches to watch their floats from under broad-brimmed hats.

A motor cycle with a small black dog riding pillion throbbed slowly past the pension and round the corner, and on the shore four ducks, stalked by an overweight cat, waddled with indecent haste towards the steps of a taverna on the left. Quacking, indignant at their loss of dignity, clumsily they mounted the steps with flapping wings and on to the taverna terrace. A fat young man with a limp appeared, shooed them away, then stretching his arms, yawned and disappeared inside again. I watched the scene for quite some while until, one by one, all left for their siestas. And suddenly the events of the past twenty-four hours caught up with me: I too sought shade and sleep.

It was almost five o'clock when I awoke. From the street below came the sound of Karpathos returning to life reminding me that the shops were reopening and that I must make provision for the morrow's breakfast. My needs were simple and did not include coffee. That I had in plenty plus a mini-boiler with a continental plug. All I required was yoghourt and fruit.

'Kalispera!' I said breezily to the backside of the owner

of a small grocery shop opposite the taverna, 'a pot of yoghourt please.' 'Oche yohourti!' she snapped continuing to bend over a crate of tinned fruit and addressing them, 'teliose – finish! Come back Sunday when the boat comes in! Or try the butcher's – he may have some.' Without straightening she pointed further up the street. 'That way,' she said. I took her advice; and drew a blank. As I did in a cheese shop and four others. Unsmilingly the heads were shaken. 'No yohourti today,' they said. 'But why?' I asked the keeper of the last shop I tried, 'Don't you make any yoghourt here?' 'Oche,' he said tetchily, 'nobody in Pigadia makes yohourti – we get it from Crete when the boat comes in.' And I had the same story when I asked for fruit – 'Come back on Sunday when the boat comes in.' It was a parody of the Geordie song but with the unspoken addendum, 'and meanwhile shut up'.

I returned to the pension clasping three small cankered apples and an equal number of stunted bananas and met Papadakis outside the shop. Solicitously he asked after my health. I told him of my lack of success. 'Ah yes,' he said, repeating the 'you-shall-have-a-fishy-on-a-little-dishy' theme, 'most of our supplies come from Crete on Sundays. We cultivate little on the island now and stocks do run low towards the weekend. Sometimes very low Even,' he added ominously, 'in the tavernas.' I began to feel apprehensive as well as hungry. 'Yes,' he counselled, 'I would suggest you went early for your meal this evening.'

'Would you recommend anywhere in particular?' I asked. Papadakis looked dubious. 'There is Yiorgo's,' he said, nodding toward the taverna opposite from which earlier the fat young man had scared away the ducks, 'but he is far from well. Nor is his mother. Or his father. Then,' he continued, turning from the hall of invalids and

'Oche yohourti! Try the butcher's.'

pointing in the direction of the harbour, 'there are one or two establishments down there. Despite the lateness of the season they are remaining open; I think.' He sounded none too confident. 'However, Mr Ebdon,' he concluded, 'do not worry about your breakfast. We have yoghourt at my home. I will bring it in the morning. And now if you will excuse me. . .'

He moved towards the doorway of the shop, then turned. 'The water is on again,' he said. And permitted himself a smile.

Grateful for this welcome intelligence and quickened by his advice, I hastened to my room, undressed, draped myself in a bath towel, and clutching my soap tablet presented myself at the showers at the end of the passage. Both were occupied. I swore under my breath, retraced my steps and spent the next five minutes filling all the available containers in the room. I had learned from bitter experience of the unpredictability of water supplies in Greece. Then, once again I prepared to return to the ablutions.

I took two steps and then stopped. Not only could I see that both were still engaged but encamped outside them, robed and be-towelled, were two figures. One was an elderly man. The other was the Proper Young Woman. Even from a distance of ten paces I could see why she was proper. Indeed, I reasoned uncharitably as I backed into my room, it was doubtful if she had ever been invited to be improper. Or would be. I sat on my bed and seethed. Nearly half an hour elapsed before I heard the sound of her feet returning down the passage; she was not only proper, but indubitably thorough.

The first stars were shining when I stood on the balcony contemplating where I should eat. Papadakis's description of the infirm Yiorgo's taverna opposite had not impressed me greatly but I could see that he was doing business. Two tables on the verandah were occupied and attended by cats. And where there were cats, I conjectured, there should be fish. I elected to go there.

I crossed the road, descended a small flight of stone steps and entered by the verandah door. There were few customers inside but of their number was the Proper Young Woman. Seated at a table in the corner she was reading a copy of *The Guardian*; and eating fish.

I walked behind the long glass-fronted display counter which divided the dining area from the kitchen. 'Kalis-perasas,' I said to Yiorgo who was stirring something in a casserole, 'ti kanete?' He grunted. 'And what,' I continued chattily in Greek, 'shall I eat tonight?'

He shrugged his shoulders. 'I don't know,' he said. And sneezed into the pot. 'Fish perhaps?' I said encouragingly. 'Finished,' said Yiorgo. And jerked his head towards *The Guardian*. I began to dislike her. 'Then what?' I asked. He sighed. 'There is meat and rice,' he said dolorously, 'and peas.'

I capitulated. 'Endaxi,' I said. 'And some retsina please.' He sighed again, hobbled to the refrigerator and brought me a bottle and a glass. I thanked him, took them to the verandah and sat down at a vacant table. Nearby, the diners I had seen from my balcony left to pay their bills, and the waiting cats leapt among the carcass-laden plates and then jumped down, each happy with a fish head or a tail. It was very frustrating.

I sat there drinking my retsina and listening to the waves, driven by a freshening wind, smacking against the verandah wall below. Ahead of me a light flashed at the end of the harbour wall, and out at sea sheet lightning lit up heavy clouds. The weather did not look at all promising.

Yiorgo's arrival at the table was heralded by a rumble of thunder. As if pulled by a magnet the cats ran towards him with twitching whiskers. Then, scenting the meal, they all turned tail. They were very wise. Far wiser than I was; but hunger drove me to desperation. Stoically I plodded through the soggy hillock of wet rice, bravely I attacked the minuscule portions of ancient sheep, and by now uncaring and accompanied by a symbolic clap of thunder overhead, spooned down the arsenal of peas. Disbelievingly the cats peered at me from the shadows and then scuttled for shelter as the first drops of heavy rain began to fall.

I hurried inside, grudgingly settled my account with Yiorgo and raced to the sanctuary of the pension. As I opened my door and switched on the light there was a simultaneous lightning flash and thunderclap and Pigadia was plunged into darkness. It seemed to me to be a particularly apposite finale to the day; and had I, when I looked through the window, seen the Four Horsemen of the Apocalypse riding across the sky in oilskins, the sight would have evoked no surprise.

I groped my way to bed and lay on it listening to the sounds of nature's fury. As storms go it was violent and short; but the tempest which raged unfettered within my stomach was no less explosive and of far greater duration.

The apostle Paul wrote that one should never allow the sun to set on one's wrath. I do not argue with his philosophy. But I was much exercised to think kindly of Yiorgo that night. . .

CHAPTER IV

The Road to Ammopi

YIORGO'S RICE wreaked havoc. Like Shakespeare's Clarence I passed a miserable night full of ugly sights and ghastly dreams. I dozed rather than slept the hours away and half heard the high-pitched whine of the dawn mosquito onslaught. I was still drowsing when my door was rapped.

'Kalimera,' said Mrs Papadakis as she entered. She put a tray on the spare bed, said 'kali orexi', and left. Her hair was still in curlers and I wondered sleepily if they were a permanent feature.

The tray had more than the promised yoghourt upon it. There was also a pot of honey and a bunch of small grapes. I thought again what kind people they were, shook myself into complete consciousness, counted the mosquito bites, and got up. It was eight o'clock. Through the windows I could see that the weather was fine. Cotton wool clouds moved slowly against a blue sky and steam was beginning to rise from the roof of the bank above Yiorgo's taverna. I turned on the tap, and the water ran; I plugged in my razor and it started to buzz. 'Jubilate,' I said as I took off the bristles, for the portents of the day seemed good. And when I won the race for the occupancy of the shower, beating the Proper Young Woman in a photo-finish, I knew that the gods were with me.

The yoghourt was excellent. I broke the thick skin, mixed in the grapes and honey and broke my fast. There is no better way of beginning a day in Greece and after two cups of instant coffee it was with a light heart that I made my way downstairs and to Papadakis's shop.

'Good morning, Mr Ebdon,' said Papadakis as I entered, half-rising from his seat behind the counter to shake hands with me, 'please sit down. I hope that you had a good night's sleep in spite of the storm?' 'Well,' I said, 'to be truthful I'm afraid I didn't.' And told him of the debacle at Yiorgo's.

Papadakis shook his head sorrowfully. 'Ah yes,' he said, 'I had feared it might be so. But Yiorgo, you must understand, has problems. He is a sad man.' The jowls quivered again. 'A very sad man,' he repeated. 'He got drunk last week and smashed up his new car on the way back from Othos. Two days, that's all he had had it. Two days.'

I made sympathetic noises. 'Did he show you his leg?' he enquired. I shook my head. 'No?' said Papadakis in surprise, 'well, he will. He shows everyone his leg. But,' he added, reassuringly, and anxious that I should know that Yiorgo enjoyed his lighter moments, 'he is not always like this. He has, as you say in English, the ups and the downs.' 'Yes,' I agreed, the steepness of Yiorgo's gradient still fresh in my mind, 'he certainly has.' 'However,' said Papadakis, dismissing the past and rolling into the present, 'today is another matter. Do you know your intentions?' 'Yes,' I said, 'I thought I would walk to Ammopi.'

Papadakis nodded approvingly but corrected my stress. 'Please,' he said, 'Ammop*i*! The accent is on the last vowel – not the first.' I thanked him for his tuition.

'Yes,' said Papadakis, leaning back in his chair and folding his hands across his stomach, 'Ammopi – The Sandy One! So beautiful there. So peaceful. And there is a taverna on the beach.' He paused to light a cigarette. 'One of our guests walks there every day to eat and swim. He has left already so you will see him there, I think.'

'Is he an elderly gentleman?' I asked, remembering the ancient I had seen by the showers the previous night. 'Very elderly,' said Papadakis solemnly, 'he is eighty-four. A German. A Mr Schalhorn.' He frowned and drew on his cigarette. 'He is also a little, how shall I say, eccentric.'

'Oh,' I said inquiringly, 'in what way?' 'He walks and talks and reads a book,' said Papadakis, as if enumerating the functions of a sophisticated doll, 'and I worry about him. I worry about him a very great deal.' 'Why?' I asked. 'Because,' said Papadakis, 'his nose and eyes are too much in the pages and not on where he is going. I am,' he said, his voice pregnant with premonition, 'most fearful for him. Also,' he continued, 'he tells me that he has found a short way down the cliffs.' He paused and leaned towards me. 'Mr Ebdon,' he said, allowing the words to drop out slowly, 'they are very steep cliffs. Very steep indeed.' And wagged his head.

'How long will it take me to get there?' I asked, both from a practical point of view and an endeavour to lighten the topic. Papadakis shrugged. 'Perhaps two hours as you do not know the way, perhaps a little less.' He coughed. 'Mr Schalhorn does it in an hour and a half,' he said; and turned his eyes to the ceiling. 'But allow me to tell you the route.'

Painstakingly he did so. I thanked him profusely for his trouble and also for the yoghourt and honey. 'Don't mention it,' he said, rising and seeing me to the door, 'there will be more for you tomorrow. And if we can do anything else for you Mr Ebdon . . . ,'

I stopped on the doorstep and turned to face him. 'As a matter of fact,' I said, 'there is one other thing I should like. Would you,' I asked, taking my courage in both hands, 'please call me Yanni? Everyone else does.' And waited.

Papadakis digested the request, then cleared his throat. 'I should,' he said, 'be pleased to.' It was, I felt, a major breakthrough.

Following Papadakis's directions I turned right past the pension, along a short street with a few small stores in it, right once more at its end, past a baker's shop with blue polythene bags of toast suspended in its window, and then left on to the steep tarmac road leading to the airport. I checked my watch to time my first walk to Ammopi. It was exactly nine o'clock.

Already the strength of the sun was making itself felt and I was grateful for the breeze which sent dust swirling around my legs as I trudged uphill with the sea to my right. I passed a cat sitting in the roadway under the stone wall of a house, eyeing an overhanging bunch of grapes. Its concentration was complete and it reminded me of the illustration of Aesop's *The Fox and The Vine*.

The way became steeper and the white-washed, shuttered houses fewer and within minutes the outskirts of the town were behind me and I looked across patches of fig and olive trees on downward slopes which ran to the sea. Up I plodded, head down as the slope increased, and noticing the brown and orange flattened corpses of locusts which had paid the penalty for flying across from one gorse-covered stretch to the other. The road was thick with their bodies and they made the surface slippery. Half a mile on I came to the first of Papadakis's landmarks, a concrete water tower on a bend in the road. Water ran from its base and trickled down the hill and a tethered panniered donkey, fly-troubled and unhappy, watched me as I turned my back on the sea and left the road to take a stone-strewn path inland.

Gradually the gradient lessened, and turning a corner around an outcrop of rocks I found myself on a plateau stretching across the peninsula. There was no shelter from the hills now and the wind which blew through a conifer plantation on my right dried the sweat which ran into my eyes from under my linen hat. I took my shirt off and let it flutter behind me as I started off along a cart track which unwound before me. Its red soil could have come from Devon and ubiquitous crickets sang in the thick gorse on either side and jumped from the centre ridge as my bare legs brushed against the long spiky grasses which grew on it.

Soon the pines gave way to fig and olive trees, and then to scrub. I strode on thinking how good it was to be alive, watching the tiny lizards in their dozens scuttle across my path, and breathing in the burnt sugar smell of wild thyme and a hundred other vegetable scents peculiar to rural untamed Greece. Twenty yards ahead a snake, warned of my approach, uncoiled itself and slithering from its basking place disappeared amongst the gorse. It reminded me to watch my step. Ten minutes further on, the track divided in a V. Possibly it was my preoccupation with the snake which made me forget Papadakis's instruction not to take the left fork but I did, wondering as I did so why suddenly there was so much broken glass underfoot and an ever-growing smell. Another five minutes' walking and the mystery was explained. I arrived at the Karpathos rubbish dump.

I could go no farther. Before me was a sheer drop and below that was the sea. To my right, a deep gorge separated the bluff of land on which I stood from the promontory on which I should have been. I had no alternative. Mocked by the garbage-hopping crows, I retraced my steps to the junction and set off again, this time in the right direction. Quite soon the scrub thinned out and the soil became stonier; and in a sandy cultivated patch wherein two poppies bloomed, stood a scarecrow with its arms at ten past eight. Propped up by a stake and executing a drunken pas seul it was beautifully dressed. A panama hat graced its pumpkin head, its shirt was black and the trousers white and I stopped to admire the artistry. But splendid though it was, it paled into insignificance compared with the sight which met me when I turned my eyes away from it.

From where it had materialized I know not, but in the near distance on what hitherto had been a deserted track, was a tall, angular figure. Head bent forward under a floppy hat and dressed in khaki shorts and shirt and with a knapsack upon its back, it moved briskly but jerkily forward, sawing the air the while with a walking stick. And unbelievably, but unmistakably, the words of Shakespeare's eighteenth sonnet were carried back to me. In a strong German accent. I had caught up with Herr Schalhorn.

What made him half turn and glance back over his left shoulder I shall never know, but he did so; and stopped in the middle of the closing couplet. His left hand held an open book. 'Good morning!' he called as I approached him, 'I

It moved briskly but jerkily forward.

recognize you! You also are staying with the good Papadakis, ya? Ya I think so.' His voice was cracked and staccato. 'I introduce myself, ya? Schalhorn!' 'Bitte,' I said, 'Ebdon.'

We shook hands. 'So,' he said, closing the book with a snap, 'you also are going to Ammopi? Good! Then we go together. It is not so far now. I should already have been there but owing to some body in my shoe I was obliged to stop for quite some time in the grasses to remove it. It was a large nail. But come!'

He was gaunt, he was old and his deeply tanned skin was wrinkled and leathery. In every particular save one, he was like an erect tortoise. The exception was his speed. He moved at twice my pace.

'Always I am doing this walk,' he cackled, as we ate up the yards, 'for three years now and reading to myself aloud.' He indicated the book. 'Today is Shakespeare, ya? Shall I compare thee to a summer day and so forth and so forth. Tomorrow will be Schiller! – then back to Shakespeare! And so on and so on.' He cackled happily. 'The good Papadakis thinks I am verrückt – nuts in the head! But no matter!' He laughed again. 'Words! Words! Words!' He glanced sideways at me through his sunglasses. 'Hamlet, ya?' And with that we came to a halt at the top of a cliff.

The panorama was breathtaking. To our right we looked down over steep gorse-covered shaly cliffs dropping suddenly to sandy lowland, and in the distance, to a perfect crescent of sandy beach in a tiny bay. On its headland stood a little church, brilliant white against the blue background of sea in yet another bay beyond it. On our left, a steep boulder-strewn path zigzagged downwards in a curving detour to the flats, ran parallel with us in the direction of the bay and then went out of sight.

'Beautiful ya?' said Schalhorn. 'Always do I look, but never do I tire.' He pointed his stick towards the bay. 'Ammopi,' he said, 'in the Bay of Amorphos; and the church is St Apostle's. And that,' he continued, nodding towards the path, 'is the way to Ammopi. But my friend, not my way. This is my way! Come!' And so saying he began clambering sideways down the cliff with all the enthusiasm of a demented crab. 'Follow me!' he cried, sending a shower of pebbles before him, 'and look out for the little stone men – the marking piles!'

I did so, marvelling at his agility, and landed hard on my rump as the shale crumbled beneath me. 'Ach!' he screeched as I rubbed my backside, 'Oh what a fall was there my countrymen and so forth – Julius Caesar, ya?' 'Yes,' I said, as I rose to my feet, 'Julius Caesar;' and prayed that I would not meet him on a Schiller day. The prospect of clattering downhill to the Ode of Joy did not appeal to me.

I made no attempt to match his rate of descent. Arms flailing and stick waving and still clutching his Shakespeare he scampered on between boulders and bushes stopping only once to replace his hat on a head as bald and white as a Leghorn's egg. He waved as he reached the earth track to Ammopi and waited for me to join him.

'Five minutes more we are there,' he pressured, 'come!' And off we set again.

The heat on the low road was like that from a furnace. Sweat poured out of me and ran down my body. Shortly the path petered out and we clambered our way over a rocky spur, down again and across a little cove, then up once more along a winding goat track and round a hairpin bend to the top of another ridge. And there, fifty feet below us, was our journey's end.

Lazy wavelets of an ebbing tide lapped gently against a slope of sand, shining and newly washed, and beyond the high water mark a stone-spattered beach backed by bushes and trees with low hanging branches led to the cane-covered verandah of a small taverna. Close at hand to its rear was a pension in the last stages of construction. A few sunbathers lay spread-eagled like starfish, and through the trees I could see one or two more sitting at tables outside the taverna, their legs resting on adjacent chairs. This, I thought, is lotus-eating land.

Schalhorn gesticulated towards the pension. 'Last year,' he barked accusingly, 'that was not here! But come!' he commanded, 'to the taverna, ya?' He stalked purposefully across the soft sand.

I was once badly frightened by a German. He caused me to leave my aeroplane abruptly and from then on I never really took to that nation. I was grateful to Schalhorn for showing me his short cut but I was glad when, having brought the taverna staff to attention, he left me to my own unorganized devices and quickly disappeared with a bottle of Henninger's to sit in the shade with his sonnets.

Swollen tongued, I introduced myself to the lady who ran the taverna together with her elderly mother and father, and asked for some water. Sympathetically they watched as I replaced the fluid I had lost en route and tut-tutted as instantly it escaped through my pores as if from a rose-sprinkler. 'Po! po! po!' they said, 'see how he sweats! Mana mu! He needs a swim!'

The lady's name was Fortula. The literal translation from the Greek is 'little light'. Fortula, however, was neither little nor light. Indeed, there was a great deal of Fortula and it spread uninhibitedly to all points of the compass; but she was very sweet and, as I discovered after I had swum, a splendid cook. Breaking my habit of midday abstinence I sat at peace with the world, a plate of tsatsiki and salad and a bottle of beer, finished them and, like Oliver Twist, asked for more.

Inside the doorway of the taverna, Fortula's mother sat peeling potatoes with arthritic fingers and tunelessly crooned to herself. Outside on a bench her husband, deep in thought, earnestly studied his left great toe, a scrawny chicken walking over imaginary broken glass picked its way hesitantly between the table legs and a brown and white mongrel scratched itself lethargically, and yawned. Time stood still.

It must have been about half past two when the calm was broken. From the direction of the nearby village set close to the main road to the airport, a taxi crawled and bumped its way down an unmade track and squealed to a halt in a cloud of dust alongside the taverna. From it emerged three figures; the taxi driver who got out slowly and stretched; and a man and woman who made their exits stiffly from the rear. The lady, who was clasping a beach bag and two rolled up grass mats, wore a floral cotton skirt over a one-piece bathing costume in navy blue, and a straw sun-hat. Her husband was attired in a maroon shirt decorated with anchors and ships and matching elasticated boxer shorts. He seemed ill at ease.

'Toilet?' he shrilled to Fortula who had appeared to greet the driver, 'toilet?' His voice was vibrant with urgency. The Greek word is very similar and Fortula beamed understandingly. 'Ne,' she said, and pointed to the back of the taverna. 'Ta,' said Knickers-to-Match, and disappeared at the double. Moments later he reappeared in a more relaxed state but paler than before his visit. 'It's not very nice, dear, I'm afraid,' he said to his wife as he relieved her of their possessions, 'not very nice at all. No.' He was a spare, middle-aged, thin-faced man with receding sandy hair and a prominent adam's-apple, and wore National Health spectacles. Instantly I recognized him and his wife as the companions of the unfortunate Gladys of the previous day. Regrettably the recognition was mutual.

'Ahha!' said Knickers-to-Match as he came towards my table and put his belongings upon it, 'we were on the plane together, were we not? Yes, I expect you remember us? With our friend? The plump lady? The one who was sick? Yes? That's right, name of Gladys. Still feeling queasy, I'm afraid, poor soul, but there we are, can't be 'elped, er helped, but –'

He broke off to greet his wife. 'Aha! there you are, dear,' he said in a tone which suggested that he was surprised to see her again, 'better now? My good lady,' he said, 'Mave to you. And I'm Les. May we join you? Ta!' And they moved in.

'Lovely weather,' said Mave. 'Yes,' I said, 'lovely.' 'Lovely,' echoed Knickers-to-Match extracting a thermos and two plastic cups from the beach bag, 'would you care to partake of a cup of tea?' Politely I declined, 'No?' said Knickers-to-Match, surprised by my refusal of such home comforts, 'well we will, won't we dear?' 'Yes,' said Mave, 'nothing like a nice cup of tea, I always say.'

Her husband unscrewed the flask, poured some of its contents into one of the cartons, and then watched in dismay as the liquid seeped through a crack in the polystyrene. 'Oh,' he said, 'we seem to have sprung a leak, dear!' And quickly poured the remainder back into the thermos. 'Funny,' he said, 'it was all right at Gatwick.' And examined the other. 'Tch!' he said, 'that's split as well!'

'Well, don't just stand there, dear,' said Mave tartly, 'go and ask in the kitchen.' Knickers-to-Match hesitated. 'Well go on,' said Mave, 'go and ask the young lady for some cups! Go on,' she insisted, 'she won't bite you!'

Reluctantly he did so and returned escorted by Fortula. 'Ta, love,' said Mave taking the cups from her; and acted as hostess. Fortula gave a little nod. 'Parakalo,' she said, 'tipotallo?' 'Ay?' said Mave, dropped on, 'what she say?' 'She's asking if you want anything else,' I said. 'Like a snack,' I hinted.

'Oh no! no! no!' said Mave hurriedly, 'we had our dinner at the hotel, didn't we dear? In Pigadeer.' 'Yes,' said Knickers-to-Match. 'Just waiting for it to go down really. Then we can have our dip.'

I translated. Fortula shrugged and moved away. 'You can't win them all,' her shoulders seemed to say; but I wondered if she had thought of charging them corkage.

Mave tasted her tea appreciatively. 'I'm looking forward to our dip,' she said, 'Um,' said Knickers-to-Match doing likewise, 'nothing like a nice dip.' Mave paused between sips. 'Somebody at the hotel,' she said, 'told me there's a place near here where they do it in the altogether.' 'Quite probably,' I said, 'it's not uncommon.' Mave stared at me. 'Disgusting,' she said, 'I wouldn't demean myself!' 'I should hope not,' said Knickers-to-Match, 'I should hope not indeed!' I hoped so too. For everyone's sake.

'Are you,' inquired Mave, 'going to have a dip?' I shook my head. 'No,' I said, 'I've had one. I'm going to start walking back to Pigadia shortly.' Knickers-to-Match's eyes bulged behind his spectacles. 'Waulk?' he said in a strangled voice, 'waulk? All the way to Pigadeer? Strewth!' 'Les!' said Mave sharply, 'don't blaspheme!'

'Nothing like a nice dip,' said Knickers-to-Match.

She took off her shirt. I was even more glad that she was not going to do it in the altogether.

From the bench by the taverna wall their taxi driver, paid and well content to wait, watched his fares prepare to take the water. So did everyone else. She oiled him and he creamed her, obeyed her instructions to blow his nose thoroughly and waited while she donned a yellow rubber bathing cap. It was a style which I had not seen since the late nineteen twenties. Then white and glistening, one fat, one thin, they made their ways to the water's edge, dabbled their toes, then waded in; and did the sidestroke.

My last sight of them was from the ridge overlooking the bay at the beginning of my return journey. They were stretched on the sand, she like a beached white whale, and he with a knotted handkerchief about his head and a paper beak on his nose. They had all the aura of day-trippers in pre-war Brighton. Blue skies and seas there may have been, and all the panoply of Greece, but where they lay, was England.

My par for the return course was just under two hours and although I had not equalled Schalhorn's time I was well pleased with my progress. The day, I reflected as I sat on the balcony after showering, had been a memorable one, full of incident and human interest. Tired but content, I watched the hills and sea grow purple as the sun sank lower in the south western sky and half listened to the faint strains of bouzoukoi music coming from a fishing boat in the harbour. It was a love song by Theodorakis, romantic and wistful, and matched the tempo of the fading light. Over the way Yiorgo, car-bereaved and lame, limped into view still carrying the cares of the world upon his shoulders and went into his kitchen. I wondered what blasphemy he would produce from his pans that evening and determined not to find out. Below me, Papadakis appeared in the roadway and looked towards the balcony. 'Good evening Mr –'

He stopped and smiled sheepishly, remembering his promise. 'Kalisperasas, Yanni' he called, 'did you have a good day?' The light glinted on his spectacles. 'I hear that you met Mr Schalhorn!' 'Yes,' I said, surprised, 'how did you know?' 'He told me,' said Papadakis, 'already he is back. He returned in a taxi with an English couple. They had been burned by the sun, Mr Schalhorn said. Also the man had been stung by a bee.'

I winced sympathetically. 'Ne,' said Papadakis, 'they gave him some ouzo to put on it; and half an onion. As you know, ouzo and onion is very good for bee stings.' I nodded. 'Ouzo is very good for everything,' I said. 'Of course,' agreed Papadakis, 'but the man's wife would not allow it. She said it made him smell.' He shrugged his shoulders. 'What can you do for such people?' he asked. And went back to his shop.

I felt sorry for Knickers-to-Match and spent the next ten minutes pondering on his misfortune and wondering where he had been attacked. I hoped for his sake that a disorientated bee, its legs heavy with sun-tan oil, had not crawled its way up his elasticated briefs; but my imagination ran riot at the thought of such a possibility. However, my musing was interrupted.

'Kalispera,' said a voice from the doorway. And on to the balcony walked a small thick-set man in his late forties with a sad, hollow-cheeked face. He could have been a professional mourner. 'Ti kanete?' he asked. 'Kala,' I said, and recognized the voice as the one which had answered Papadakis from the depths of the lavatory during my conducted tour of the pension. 'Manoli?' 'Ne!' he confirmed. 'And your name I think is Yanni? Ne! I heard the old man talking to you. And this,' he said, turning to another figure who had appeared and was forking something out of a tin, 'is my colleague, Stephano.' 'Yasu!' said Stephano, extending the fork to me, '– have a sardine!'

'Epharisto,' I said; and took it from the prongs. 'Good eh?' inquired Stephano who was a podgy young man with bulging eyes under heavy black brows; and engulfed two more. 'Verra, verra good!' he emphasized. And demolished another. 'My friend,' said Manoli, lighting a cigarette, 'is very fond of fish.'

Stephano closed his eyes in ecstasy and still clasping the fork between two fingers, blew a kiss towards heaven. 'Orea!' he husked, 'pu orea! – quite beautiful!' Returning from Elysium he peered into the empty tin. 'Teliose,' he said – 'finish!' And poured the oil over the balcony. 'I get more,' he said, putting the container in the ashtray; and vanished.

Manoli drew on his cigarette. 'That one,' he said, exhaling, 'is like a cat. A tom-cat,' he added. 'That is why he eat so much fish. He says it makes him vigorous.'

'Ne!' roared Stephano reappearing and unwinding a fresh tin of sardines, 'plenty strong! Good for girls! Not half I should say,' he continued in pidgin English; and rolled his eyes. 'Ha! Ha!' he said throatily; and flexed his right arm.

'Stephano,' said Manoli who had no English but a ready understanding of mime, 'is very proud of his strength. Which is why he is unhappy here. Here he cannot find a girl.'

'True,' said Stephano making an onslaught on the new

tin, 'two months and no girls! All work! No fun! This place like necrotophia – cemetery. Thanks God we soon go Athens!' Mournfully he selected another sardine and chewed at it in silence. I wondered why in the absence of any outlet for his carnal appetite he took in so much aphrodisiac. Unless he was keeping himself in trim for his return to the capital he seemed to me to be verging on the masochistic.

Manoli broke the silence. 'Do you like fish?' he enquired. 'Very much,' I said, 'but I couldn't get any last night.' And nodded towards Yiorgo's. 'I ate there,' I said. 'Ah,' said Manoli, 'there is a better place. Near the harbour. We will show you. There one can eat swordfish and barbunia.' 'Ne!' endorsed Stephano, jettisoning the second tin and licking his fingers, 'barbunia! barbunia! Viva barbunia!' And blew fish-tainted kisses with both hands.

Manoli stubbed out his cigarette in the sardine tin. 'Stephano eats barbunia every day,' he said. 'Sometimes twice a day. You know this fish?' he asked. 'Ne,' I said, 'red mullet. It is very good.' 'The best!' shouted Stephano rhapsodically, and drummed his chest with his fists. 'You come, ne? Tonight! With us!' 'Endaxi,' I said, 'epharisto!' 'Bravo!' said Stephano shaking me warmly by the hand and transferring a good deal of sardine oil in the process, 'but now, ouzo.' 'Ne,' agreed Manoli, let us go and drink some ouzo. It is good for the appetite.' 'And,' said Stephano, suppressing a burp, 'for the digestion.'

Stephano and Manoli were a nice if strangely assorted couple. Their names, I thought, would make good billing on a music hall poster advertising a double act. They were, I discovered, as we lingered over an ouzo, two of a team of Post Office engineers engaged in maintenance work on the island. Presently they were working in Aperi and would be going there early in the morning. If I wished to go with them in their transport I would be welcome to do so. It was a pretty village, they said, and I should see it. Moreover, Stephano advised me, keeping things in perspective, one could get barbunia there. 'Bravo,' he said when I accepted their offer; and patted his stomach. 'Barbunia!' The mention of the word triggered afresh his gastric juices and reminded him that a full hour had passed since his last intake of fish. Like Samson after Delilah had had a go with the scissors he felt his strength ebbing. 'Should we not go now,' he inquired anxiously of Manoli, 'to eat?' Manoli smiled indulgently. 'Endaxi,' he said. 'Ella.' And we made our way towards the harbour.

'I hope,' said Manoli as we came to a halt outside the glass door of the taverna, 'that She is in a good mood.' 'She?' I asked. 'Tassia,' said Manoli, 'the owner. She is a strange woman. They tell me she was once married to an Ethiopian but he went to sea and never came back.' He clicked his tongue and raised his eyebrows. 'Anyway,' he said, 'let us find out.' 'Ne,' said Stephano, impatient for the off; and led the way in.

The taverna was small, crowded with locals and noisy with chatter but one voice rose distinctively above the hubbub. Sandpaper in texture it belonged to a strikingly handsome olive-skinned woman with features like Nefertiti's but unfortunately, with teeth like Ramases the Second's. She recognized my companions as we made our way towards a vacant table and screamed a welcome to them. 'Endaxi,' confided Manoli as I took my seat, 'all is well. She is in a good temper; and so, I think, is her son.'

He pointed to a remarkably good-looking boy in his late teens with black curly hair and dark skin who was clearing some dishes from a nearby table. 'Sometimes,' he said, 'they fight like cat and dog.' 'Ne,' agreed Stephano, 'bam! bam! bam! And so does the daughter.' He inhaled noisily through his nostrils and clenched both his fists. 'Grrhh!' he said. And exhaled through his teeth. 'Plenty sexful, my God!' he exclaimed. And went into the kitchen. He returned shortly carrying three glasses and an equal number of opened retsina bottles. 'There is,' he said, addressing Manoli, and filling the glasses, 'only a kilo of barbunia left. Just one kilo. So I have ordered swordfish for you and Yanni. Endaxi?' He banged his tumbler on the table. 'Stinyamas!' he said, effectively preventing any opposition to his unilateral action, 'cheers!'

As Stephano had said, the daughter was very sexful. He looked hungrily at her when she brought us a large salad as a precursor to the fish. 'Po! po! po!' he said, his eyes upon her as she moved back to the kitchen with her hips swaying, 'what buttocks!' And speared an onion. I wondered what he would be like after a kilo of barbunia: privately I debated also his ability to consume such an amount; but he did so. With ease.

It was a good meal and in the fashion of the Greeks we spent some time enjoying it. Fresh and continuous supplies of retsina liberated tongues and encouraged conversation which varied from discussion on the belief in the risen Christ to the problem of traffic congestion in general and of that in Oxford Street in particular. Stephano recently had been in that vicinity. 'Aah,' he moaned, moved by the remembrance of half-clad dummies in Selfridges' windows, 'ah, the English girls! Po! po! po!' He raised his glass toward Tassia's daughter who was hovering seductively by the sink. 'S'agapo!' he said thickly and spilling much of its contents in the upward motion, 'I love you!' Tassia's daughter looked at him dispassionately and thrust her open palm towards him. 'Pera! pera!' she said, 'all the way!'

'You see?' said Stephano mournfully, 'always same thing – piss off!' He sighed and got up from the table. 'Toilet,' he enlightened us. Manoli watched him go and picked his teeth. 'That one,' he said, examining the toothpick, 'should be doctored.' And poured some more retsina.

It was close on eleven o'clock when we left. Mama Barbunia, as I had dubbed Tassia, bade us a cheerful goodnight and said that she hoped she would see us on the morrow. 'Of course,' said Stephano, 'for barbunia!' Again the word acted as a stimulus and he started to sing. His voice was as flat as a plaice but at least his spirits had been restored and by the time we reached the pension he was in very good form.

Manoli paused with his hand on their bedroom door-handle. 'Peraste,' he said, 'come in; for a cognac.' 'Ne,' said Stephano putting his hand in the small of my back and propelling me into the room, 'and for music!' 'Music?' I said. 'Ne,' said Manoli as Stephano produced a bottle of Metaxa brandy and glasses; and unearthed an accordion from under his bed. 'Kathiste,' he said, 'sit down.' And unstrapping the instrument he allowed its bellows to fill. He was no mean performer and it was a thousand pities that his recital was destined to end as abruptly as it did.

It was half-way through a stirring song eulogizing the exploits of sponge fishermen from the island of Kalymnos when the interruption happened. There was an imperious rapping at the door. 'Peraste!' yelled Stephano from where he was lying on his bed and continuing to beat time with his brandy glass, 'and welcome!'

'Some of us wish to get some sleep!'

Sharply the door was flung open and there, like an avenging angel, stood the Proper Young Woman. Her hair was tied back in a pony tail and she was wearing seersucker pyjamas, large pink-framed glasses and an expression of fury. 'Mana mu!' muttered Manoli as he took in the horrid spectacle; and allowed the accordion to wheeze into silence. 'Some of us,' shrilled the Proper Young Woman and without a preliminary warm up, 'wish to get some sleep!'

Ouzo-ed, barbunia-ed, retsina-ed and cognac-ed but patently with impaired vision and dressed only in a string vest and his underpants Stephano leapt from his bed and careered towards her. 'Ne!' he roared, 'ella, cukla mu – come 'ere doll!' and opened his arms to embrace her.

The sound of her hand meeting his face must have been heard on Rhodes. 'And you,' she added, adjusting her spectacles and recognizing me as Stephano pirouetted from the force of the blow, 'should be ashamed of yourself!' And so saying she slammed the door shut, and flounced out.

There was a moment's silence followed by a long sigh from the accordion as Manoli squeezed the air from it. 'I think,' he said as he re-buckled it, 'that perhaps we ought to go to bed.' I nodded in agreement. 'At what time shall we meet to leave for Aperi?' I asked. 'Eight o'clock,' said Manoli. 'Endaxi,' I said, 'kalinichta. And sweet dreams,' I called to Stephano who was applying a wet flannel to his face before a mirror. He turned towards me. 'Pera! pera!' he said. And I did. And, as recorded in the book of Genesis, 'so ended the second day.'

CHAPTER V

Telephone and Other Exchanges

C ONTRARY TO GREEK tradition Manoli was punctual the
following morning. At eight o'clock precisely he
appeared outside the pension in a taxi. Ten minutes
later, and in answer to the blaring of the horn, Stephano
materialized looking distinctly shop-soiled, and we drove
away. Nor was he communicative during the twenty
minute uphill journey to Aperi but spent much of his time
fingering the right side of his face. Until then I had not
realized that the Proper Young Woman was a south paw.
The taxi driver eyed him in his driving mirror.

'That's a nasty bruise you have there,' he said conversationally, 'how did it happen?' Stephano remained
silent but Manoli's narrative, suitably embroidered, lasted
until we reached the outskirts of Aperi. The taxi driver
found the account vastly entertaining. 'I know that one,'
he said, 'I brought her from the airport last week. She
leaves this afternoon.' He glanced again at Stephano's
image in the mirror and chuckled throatily. 'My God!' he
said 'you must be desperate! For me? Not even with a
sack over her head . . .'

He was still enjoying the incident when we pulled up on the slope outside a telephone exchange. 'Endaxi,' said Manoli, getting out first, 'this is where we start to work.' He pointed towards a small flight of concrete steps leading to the basement of the building. 'If you would like to look at Aperi for an hour or so and then return, you will find us in a room down there.' 'Endaxi,' I said. And leaving them about their business I started to walk uphill.

It was a steep winding climb before I reached a high vantage point beyond the upper limits of the village but the effort was well worth while. Aperi lay at my feet facing the blue waters of Vronti Bay in the far distance and looking more like a hill village in Tuscany than one in Greece. I looked down on tiers of sloping terracotta roofs of two storeyed, balconied houses painted in creams and greens, all obviously cared for and maintained, and each with a forecourt planted with orange and medlar and lemon trees. Also, I noticed, the many new buildings in various stages of completion faithfully followed the traditional style of architecture. Dollars from expatriate Greeks were purchasing the materials and labour but here there was no sign of New World brashness. Tradition was strong in Aperi.

There was an air of pride and quiet prosperity about the village and the aura became more apparent as I walked back down the hill, then along the narrow stone pathways which separated the houses. Even the cats which peeped suspiciously at me from around the corners of buildings were well fed and sleek. I passed by whitewashed roughcast walls topped with metal railings over which blue Morning Glory and magenta bougainvillaea spilled; I peered through ornamental iron gates at tidy gardens and vine-shaded patios and looked in admiration at the decoration on balconies and facades; and everywhere I smelt fresh paint.

I meandered farther downhill, past this house and that, zigzagging as the paths dictated until eventually the buildings thinned out and I found myself on an earth track leading to the main road at the commencement of Aperi. Below me, on my left, water from a spring trickled down a course in the hillside and ran into a drinking trough set in a clearing off the road. Opposite it in the lee of the hill was a large building with long tall windows. In another setting it could have been mistaken for a Methodist Hall. I stopped for a moment wondering what it was, and to listen to the music of the water as it gurgled on its way. Despite the early hour the morning was very hot and the sight and sound of it aggravated my thirst.

A man came out of the building carrying a yellow plastic pail and crossed to fill it from the outlet. Halfway on his return journey he looked up and saw me. 'Kalimera!' he shouted. 'Poo parte?' 'Nowhere in particular,' I called back, 'but I'm very thirsty.' He nodded in understanding and pointed to the track on which I stood. 'Follow that to the road,' he instructed, 'turn left and you are here. Endaxi?' 'Epharisto,' I shouted; and followed his directions. Five minutes later I cupped my hands under the water flow and drank. It was cold and pure. 'Kalo, ne?' said an approving voice behind me. I flicked the water from my palms and turned to face the speaker. It was the man I had seen with the pail. 'Very good,' I agreed. He grunted. 'German?' he asked. 'Oche,' I said, 'Anglos.' He grunted again. 'Endaxi,' he said, 'come in for an ouzo.' And led the way to the building.

I consulted my watch. At nine-thirty in England I reflected, I would have looked askance had I been invited to start on the hard stuff. Here, the suggestion seemed quite proper; and clearly the place was not a Methodist Hall.

'Kathiste,' said my host when we got inside, 'sit down.' He pointed to a table at which was seated a heavily jowled and pock-marked man in his early sixties drinking coffee. 'My uncle,' he said. And went behind a bar. 'Hiya,' said Uncle extending a work-worn hand piebald with liver spots, 'park your ass.' I obliged him. 'You from London, England?' he inquired in thick American and wheezing badly as his nephew brought the ouzo. I told him I was; and why I was in Aperi; and for how long. 'Me,' he said slurping the last of his coffee, 'I gotten back from Pittsburgh last fall. Worked there for forty years. In the mines.' He coughed bronchially. 'Jeez,' he gasped when the spasm passed, 'dust, I reckon.' And wiped his eyes. He watered his ouzo turning it into milk. 'Good place, the U.S. if you keep your head,' he said; 'and your money.' He raised his glass. 'I kept both,' he said. And chuckled. 'Yes sirree! Gotten a good house here, no problems moneywise, and a reserved place in the boneyard. Yes sir! Wouldn't croak in no place else!'

He looked at me quizzically. 'Wadja make of Aperi then?' I said I thought it was very beautiful and remarked on the continued lines with tradition. 'O.K.,' he said, 'and that's the way we wanna keep it. Begging your pardon John, we don't want no goddam tourists here – leastwise not too many. No sir!' He started to cough again and took another sip at his ouzo. 'Seen the school,' he asked, 'close by where your friends are working?' I nodded. 'Great place,' said Uncle. 'Only High School in the island.' His lungs started to bubble once more. 'And you know where they gotten the money to build that?' He tapped his chest. 'From me,' he said, 'and all the other folk in America – all the way from the U.S.A.!' He wheezed again and finished his drink. 'Maybe mazuma ain't everything,' he said, 'but it sure helps.'

He got up heavily and held out his hand. 'Nice knowing you, John. See you around.' He moved slowly to the door with the aid of a stick and paused at the exit. 'Have a good day,' he said. And went out.

I turned towards the nephew who was leaning on the bar and gazing after his uncle with pale blue deep-set haunted eyes which pierced the distance, and thanked him for his hospitality. He had gaunt features flanked by thick black mutton chop whiskers and belonged to another century. I had seen his face in the Retreat From Moscow – one of Napoleon's disillusioned soldiery. 'Your father's brother?' I asked. 'Ne,' he said, 'he is a good man. He has everything; except his health.' 'And did your father emigrate as well?' I pursued. 'Oche,' he said, reaching for a packet of Karelia and lighting one, 'he stayed.' He drew hard upon his cigarette until it glowed. 'I never knew my father,' he said. 'He was shot by the Germans.'

I talked with him for a while and then took my leave and walked thoughtfully back towards the telephone exchange. In the space of forty minutes, I reflected, I had been made aware of much of the social history of Karpathos. And one short sentence had reminded me that it was not so long ago that fear had stalked the villages of the Dodecanese and blood had been spilt in the hills.

Manoli was standing outside the building when I reached it, mopping his face with a handkerchief. 'It is like an oven down there,' he said jerking his head towards the basement, 'I've just come up for air.' 'Where's Stephano?' I asked. 'Working,' said Manoli, 'and sweating. But feeling better I think. Go and see him.' 'Endaxi,' I said; and went down the steps and into the small nerve centre of the exchange.

As Manoli had said, it was sweltering inside. In the centre of the tiny narrow box of a room, and facing a wall panelled with the paraphernalia of a modern telecommunications system, stood Stephano, shirtless, damp and rather smelly. 'Yasu Yanni!' he said as I joined him, 'now you see all things for telephone speech – for everywhere and all peoples. Verra verra good, yes?' I told him I was impressed but understood nothing of these mysteries. Electronics and electricity I admitted had always frightened me and I would rather stay in the dark than change a fuse. 'Not worry!' said Stephano patting me patronizingly, 'you know plenty other thing! Like blah blah blah with Bibbysee! Verra good!' His recognition of my ability with a microphone aroused a fresh line of thought.

'You want speak?' he asked, beaming at me and deftly disconnecting a meter, 'you can! Anywhere in world! Free! No problem!' He waggled a hand receiver enticingly in front of me. Quickly I thought of friends and relations in far flung stations who might welcome my voice but apart from an aged great-aunt in a nursing home in Ilkley I could think of nobody. 'Oche,' I said, 'tipota.' 'O.K.,' said Stephano, 'but wait.' He produced a diary from his hip pocket and turned to a well thumbed page of telephone numbers. 'Ne,' he said, finding the one he wanted, 'now I speak to girlfriend in Sid-en-ham. Lourrine!' He savoured the lady's name and closed his eyes. She verra verra beautiful! And,' he added, 'she love me too much!'

The ensuing dialogue was brief but fascinating.

'Allo darleeng!' he husked into the mouthpiece, 'ow har you darleeng? I kees you yes? All hover! Wat?' A voice

crackled from the other end of the line. 'Wat? he repeated.
The crackling intensified. Stephano took the receiver from
his ear and looked puzzled. 'No understand,' he said, 'too
quick speaking. Please – you talk.' Reluctantly I took the
instrument from him and cleared my throat. 'Hello,' I said.
'Oos that?' shrilled a very common voice. I elaborated.
'You speak Greek?' asked the voice with a distinct edge to
it. 'Yes,' I said. 'Well tell him to get stuffed then,'
instructed the voice, 'randy beast.' And hung up.

'Wat say?' said Stephano anxiously as I handed him the
receiver. I did not have the heart to tell him. 'I think,' I said,
'that she is very busy. Also,' I lied, 'there may be a fault in
Sydenham.' Stephano nodded. 'I try again,' he said, 'no
problem'; and sighed. 'I meet her Athens this year,' he
confided. 'Highclass, ne? Poli highclass.'

The appearance of Manoli saved me from committing
perjury for the second time. 'Ella,' he called from the
doorway; and beckoned us outside. 'Listen,' he said. From
up the hill came the sound of the tsabouna – a wind
instrument not unlike the bagpipes, and a man singing.
Louder and louder grew the noise as the performers drew
nearer and then into sight came four figures, each
following the other like a line of dancing ducks –
spearheaded by the piper. Second in line was a bouzoukoi
player, then came the vocalist who was waving a bottle
over his head and the rear was brought up by another man
similarly engaged. Floral-shirted and all unshaven, down
the hill they danced in unison, two steps forward and one to
the left, two more forward and one to the right, blowing,
plucking, singing, drinking, flushed with effort and with
wine, they passed below us on a curve and swayed and
capered to the nearby school.

They danced two circuits of its playground and then

came to a halt in the centre. And from the school building, as if at a signal, poured fifty girls dressed in blue and white. Hopping and skipping towards the quartet, quickly they formed a circle round them and danced a full half-hour away to the pipes and strings and clapping hands while the singer twirled in their midst. Then as suddenly as they had appeared, off went the troop still playing and singing, past us and up the hill again, out of sight and sound.

I felt I was watching a dream sequence; that all the girls should have been Pied-Pipered into the hills, never to return; but the scene was real enough. 'Does anything like that happen in England?' asked Manoli as we watched the pupils disperse. I shook my head. 'No,' I said, 'never.' None the less, the possibility of such a happening awakened my imagination. It would be interesting, I thought, to see what the reaction would be if a group of inebriated Morris dancers suddenly cavorted into the quadrangles of Benenden or Cheltenham Ladies' College.

Shortly after the divertissement and when we had all drunk cups of thick Greek coffee at an adjacent cafeneon, Manoli and I returned to Pigadia leaving Stephano to continue the day's work in another village. I wondered if he would try to establish contact with Sydenham again and hoped for his sake that he would not do so. I doubted if his ego would admit to much more battering.

As we emerged from the taxi outside the pension, the Proper Young Woman, armed with a suitcase and a string bag was saying goodbye to Papadakis. She glared at Manoli when she saw him. 'Kalo taxithe,' he said courteously, 'have a good journey.' The P.Y.W. clutched her string bag convulsively and snorted. 'Huh!' she said. And tossing her head she picked up her suitcase and stalked towards a waiting cab.

Soberly Papadakis watched her go and then addressed Manoli. 'It is not everyone, Mr Manoli,' he said reproachfully, 'who enjoys accordion music. Particularly late at night. Also,' he continued, as one approaching a graveside, 'I should be grateful if you made sure that your colleague controlled himself. At all hours.' 'Endaxi,' said Manoli contritely, and made towards the stairs. 'See you this evening,' I called after him. 'Of course,' said Manoli over his shoulder and went on his way. Papadakis turned to me. 'Mr Zagorianos telephoned early this morning,' he said. 'There has been a change of plan. He is coming by air and not by ferry. My son has gone to meet him. And,' he added, 'Mrs Zagorianos will not be with him.' 'Oh?' I said, surprised, 'why not?' 'I don't know,' said Papadakis, 'but he said he looked forward to seeing you.'

It was mid afternoon when George appeared. I saw his arrival from the balcony and watched as Papadakis came out to embrace him. I called out and looking up he returned my wave. 'I'll be with you in an hour,' he said, 'business;' and the two men went into the shop. Five minutes later I witnessed the return of Stephano. It was not a happy sight. Slamming the door of his taxi and paying off the driver he moved quickly towards the entrance attended by an imaginary black cloud. I listened to him taking the stairs two at a time, heard him burst in upon Manoli and marvelled at the strength of his voice. Muffled and unintelligible though it was it was clear that once again the fates had dealt him a heavy blow.

The narrative continued for some time, Stephano's voice rising and falling like an angry sea and backed towards its end by the sound of Manoli's accordion. I wondered if Schalhorn had told him that music soothed the savage beast and that mindful of Papadakis's admonition he was doing his best; but I was glad that the Proper Young Woman had left.

Eventually the furore, both vocal and musical, died down. Shortly after its cessation Manoli joined me on the balcony. He looked jaded. 'You heard?' he asked, more as a formality than a genuine enquiry. 'Yes,' I said, 'I did. What was the matter?' Manoli sucked his teeth. 'In a word,' he said, 'barbunia. He couldn't get any for his lunch. Also,' he continued, exploring a cavity with his index finger and studying the extracted trophy, 'he had bad news from England. On the telephone. He is not very happy.' 'No,' I said under my breath as Stephano slouched into view with his hands thrust deep into his trouser pockets and still looking like thunder, 'he certainly is not.'

Stephano hooked a metal framed chair into position with his foot and slumped into it. He glowered at me. 'Lourrine,' he said darkly, 'she tell me – go-to-hell! Also she say, get stuffed.' He stared moodily in front of him and then at me. 'I know go-to-hell,' he said, 'but wat, get stuffed?' 'Ine to idio,' said George, coming through the doorway, 'the same thing! Yasu Yanni mu!'

We greeted each other and I effected introductions all round. 'But what of Anna-Marie?' I asked of George when he had been appraised of Stephano's lovelife and dietary requirements and had made sympathetic noises, 'why isn't she with you?' George looked at his fingernails. 'Cats,' he said softly, 'she did not think it too wise to leave them. They are not so good.'

'Like Wednesday night?' I asked, the incidents still fresh in my memory. 'Worse,' said George. And enlightened the others. 'So you see, my friend,' he concluded and addressing Stephano, 'we all have our problems. With some of us it is women, with others, cats.' 'And both,' said

Manoli, preparing to go, 'have claws.' He smiled wryly. 'We all meet later, yes? For a meal?' 'Endaxi!' said Stephano, rising and brightening visibly as he followed Manoli, 'at Mama Barbunia's!'

CHAPTER VI

Frustration, Elation and Big Fat Finns

EVEN BEFORE WE reached the taverna we were promised that the evening would be an interesting one.

From within the establishment came the sound of raised voices and breaking crockery. Then, as we drew level with it, the door was flung open and out staggered Mama Barbunia's son. He was followed closely by a plate and a stream of invective. Momentarily he stood his ground and returned the abuse before storming off in the direction of the harbour. Inside, and holding the centre of the ring, stood his mother, hands on hips and breathing heavily and saying things that no mother should say to a son. Ever. But whatever the fight had been about, plainly she had gained a majority verdict from her customers. Excluding her daughter who was weeping into a dishcloth, they were behind her to a man; the cheers were deafening.

'Kalisperasas,' said Manoli as we entered the arena in line astern, 'ti kanete?' 'Kalispera,' she snapped back, 'ti thelis – what do you want?' 'Barbunia!' cried Stephano, his arms outstretched, 'what else!' 'Oche barbunia!' she snarled, and rushed back to her stove.

Stephano stopped in his tracks as if pole-axed. '*Oche barbunia?*' he repeated hoarsely, his eyes bulging with disbelief, 'oche *barbunia?*' 'Oche!' she screamed through a haze of smoking fat, 'tipota! Teliose!' 'Ne!' cackled an elderly man at a nearby table holding up a backbone in either hand and dangling them before him, 'teliose!' 'Sosta!' confirmed his companion doing likewise, 'teliose!'

It was the last straw. Stephano stared at them, his fists clenching and unclenching. 'Aaah!' he said, and made a bee-line for the door. Reaching it he turned, and facing his tormentors drew on his recent acquisition to his English vocabulary. 'Get stuffed!' he said. And vanished into the night.

'I think,' said George, as he watched Stephano make his exit, 'that we should have something to drink.' 'I agree,' said Manoli, 'it will give her time to calm down. Also,' he added eyeing the daughter who was still engaged in mopping-up operations with the dishcloth, 'I think we help ourselves.'

Manoli was right. After we had destroyed three bottles of retsina, inviting Mama B. to assist us in the emptying of the third, she proved less intransigent and we placed our order. One bottle more and the mezes arrived. And so did Knickers-to-Match. With his wife. Both resembled boiled lobsters and both were peeling. However, there was no visual evidence of where the incensed bee had struck.

'Aha!' said Knickers-to-Match coming over to us and sounding even more like a strangulated counter-tenor, 'so we meet again, do we not!' 'Yes,' I said, my heart sinking, 'we do, don't we? How's the sting?' 'Er, better, ta,' said Knickers-to-Match, instinctively feeling the afflicted spot, 'but still swollen. I think it must have been an 'ornet, er hornet. Very nasty, yes, However,' he continued and winning the battle with another aspirate, 'this is quite an adventure for us, we haven't ventured to partake of a meal outside the hotel yet, no. But as I said to Mave this afternoon, after tea, I said, well, I said, I think it's time we tried the local food. After all, I said, nothing venture nothing gain and we don't want to go back to Hanwell without 'aving heaten, er eaten, local food, didn't I, dear?' Unenthusiastically Mave confirmed the statement.

'And so,' said Knickers-to-Match, adjusting his spectacles, 'here we are. But might I inquire of what you are partaking – if you don't think me rude, that is?' 'Not in the least,' I said, 'I'm glad to be of help.' And pointed to the nearer of two dishes. 'That's tsatsiki,' I advised him. 'It's cucumber and oil and yoghourt and garlic, and the other,' I explained, 'is skorthia – a mixture of bread paste and oil and garlic. I shall dip my soupea in it when it comes.' 'Dip your what into it?' asked Mave in a startled voice. 'My soupea,' I repeated – 'cuttlefish.' Mave stared at me disbelievingly. 'What, like you give budgies?' she said. 'It's squid,' said George flatly as Mama Barbunia brought it to the table, 'and very good it is.' Knickers-to-Match bent forward and peered at the plate dubiously. 'Oh,' he said. 'I see. Yes. H'mm.' And wrinkled his nose. The gesture did not pass unnoticed.

Mama Barbunia glared at him and bridled. 'What's the matter with him?' she inquired, 'is there something wrong with my cooking?' Hurriedly we assured her that it was perfect; and explained. 'Huh!' said Mama Barbunia, and wiped her hands on her apron. 'Anyway,' she rasped, 'what does he want?' We translated.

Knickers-to-Match swallowed hard. 'Well,' he said, still mesmerized by the squid and consulting his wife, 'it's hard to say really, isn't it dear? But could you ask our good lady here if she could do sausage and eggs – twice?'

Considering the amount of stress which she had undergone, I thought Mama Barbunia's reply most temperate. But I did not see Knickers-to-Match in there again.

And so the days passed, and all too quickly. George completed his business and returned to Rhodes on the following Monday, Schalhorn departed on the Wednesday, and by Thursday night Stephano had recovered from his barbunia withdrawal symptoms. Daily I walked to Ammopi and swam in the warm clear waters of its enchanting bay; and nightly in company with Manoli, I braved the uncertainty of Mama Barbunia's temper. Four times I saw the day grow light at dawn and watched the great red sun turn to shimmering gold as it climbed higher in pursuit of fleecy cloud, warming the air and land; I saw seven sunsets, each more exquisite than the one before but all flushing the sea with mother-of-pearl and the cliffs and sky with pink. From the harbour's end at twilight I watched endless elliptical bands of twittering swallows fly from a little white chapel on the cliffs to skim the waves and then return. And through Manoli I made new friends.

There were a number of other Post Office engineers working on the island and based in Pigadia. Some came from Crete, others from Athens and three from the Peloponnese. In ones and twos I met them all, over ouzo or an evening meal and many a happy time we had. But it was my last night in Karpathos that I remember with particular affection.

Twelve of us, including one wife named Katrina who was possessed of a powerful voice and an equally vigorous three year old called Michaeli, set off in two cars of dubious roadworthiness for the hill village of Othos. The advance guard had left about an hour before us in a Post Office van complete with Manoli, his accordion and a bottle of ouzo, and entirely surrounded by cable. By the time we reached the taverna, the proceedings were well under way.

At the head of a long table covered with eatables and bottles, Manoli was squeezing away for dear life, while a minute dark beady-eyed Athenian named Apostoli with long black curling moustachios and the highest voice I had ever heard, was standing on a chair with his arms outstretched and his mouth wide open and ouzo coming out of his ears. 'Ella!' they cried as we made our entrance, and we all sat down and joined in the song while the bottles clinked and the glasses were filled and food was speared on to forks. Uninhibitedly we sang, with Apostoli leading the field. Unmindful of solids but attentive to all fluids within his reach, his voice rose higher and higher until I feared for his well-being. Eventually the strain told on him. Crossing his eyes he fell off his chair and went to sleep, like the dormouse in Alice; but nobody tried to put him in a teapot. Instead, a Nikos and an Evangelos with iron grey hair and a face like a hawk, and a puckish sense of humour reseated him and then smiling happily at each other across him, cradled his head in their arms and carefully tied his moustachios together with one of my shoelaces.

'Po! Po! Po!' bellowed Katrina over the cheers and applause, 'bravo!' And stuffing a spiced sausage into the mouth of little Michaeli who had become over-excited during the pantomime, she stepped into the breach left by the stricken Apostoli and the revels continued.

It was after midnight when we started back to Pigadia, still singing and with Apostoli still comatose. Later, he was carried away by Evangelos and other helpers and put to bed, his moustachios still tied together, and we all parted

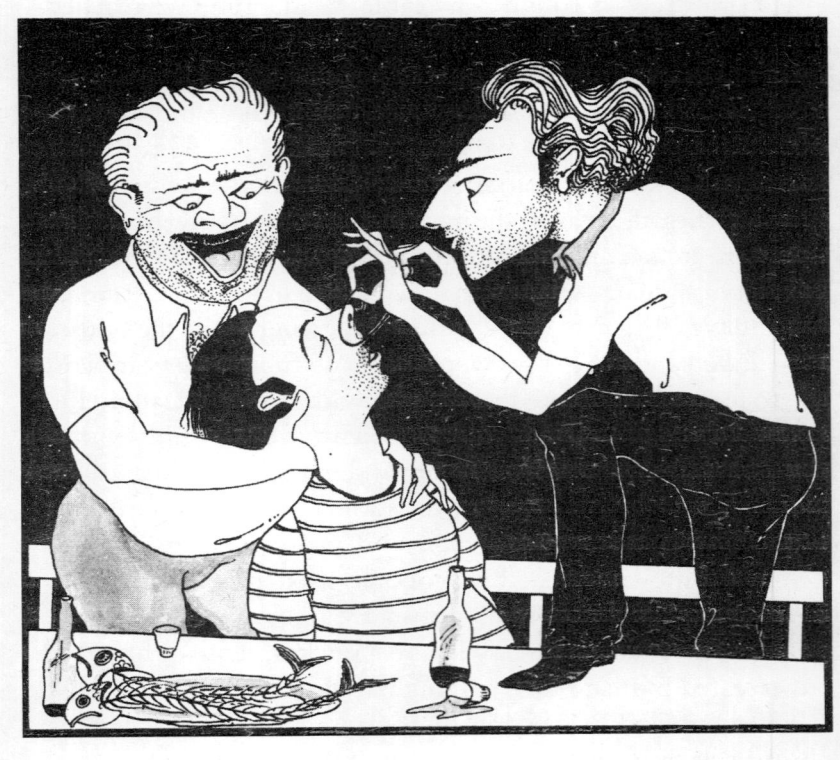

Carefully tied his moustachios together.

company. I wondered what his reaction would be when he awoke in the morning.

The night was clear and very beautiful, and I had no immediate wish for bed. I walked slowly down to the harbour, filling my pipe as I went, along to the end of the jetty, and sat on its wall. The stones still held the heat of the day and I stayed there for quite some while, smoking and listening to the waves as they ran over the shingle and rolled the pebbles. On the quay, cats squabbled over some discarded fish-heads and I could hear Mama Barbunia cursing as she swept out her taverna. There was the sound of tinkling glass as she put her broom handle through one of the small windows and her eloquence reached new heights. Clearly she had had a very long and tiring day and I hoped for their sakes that during the evening to come nobody would ask for sausage and eggs once, let alone twice.

Over the chapel on the cliffs with its adjoining cemetery where during the war, so I was told, two shepherds had been forced to dig their own graves and were then shot by their German masters, Orion the Hunter shone brilliantly against a moonless sky. Before the fainter stars of his curved shield the lowered Bull's head of the Hyades charged down upon him in a vengeful V, while higher still the Pleiades, the lovely Seven Sisters, flashed firefly blue as they fled before him. And at my back, the Great and Little Bears prowled round the Pole, ever watchful of Orion – Callisto and Arcas as they were, until they were changed into beasts. Or so the story goes.

So many of the legendary figures of Ancient Greece were in the skies that night. Perseus and Pegasus, Taurus, Andromeda, heroes and heroines, men and beasts, all were there in the stars. And I thought of the days when the

Greek gods reigned and placed them there in the sky; when the Earth was round but did not move, but all around it did; when the universe was a nest of spheres and Man was at its centre. And I thought too of the words of Homer, written centuries before.

'Therein be fashioned the earth,' he wrote, 'therein the heaven, therein the sea and the untiring sun and the full moon, therein the marvels with which the heaven is crowned, the Pleiades and the Hyades and the mighty Orion and the Bear which they also call the Wain, that turneth ever in her place and watcheth Orion, and hath no part in the baths of Ocean.'

I knocked out my pipe and began to wander back. Man's conception of the universe, I reflected, had changed greatly since Achilles' shield was emblazoned with the seven stars of the Bear; but not so the beauty of a Grecian sky. That has remained constant. And, thank God, it always will be so.

That afternoon I said goodbye to Papadakis, caught the little plane to Rhodes and stayed the night with the Zagorianoses before returning to England. Knickers-to-Match was in the same aircraft. He was still peeling.

'And how,' inquired George over supper, 'was Mama Barbunia when you left?' 'Coming to the boil again,' I said. We laughed and enlightened Anna-Marie. 'But the island,' she asked anxiously, 'you liked the island, Yanni, yar?' 'Indeed I did,' I said. Anna-Marie sighed. 'Yar, yar,' she said, closing her eyes, 'it is so so bew-ti-ful! So, so alive with der nai-char, yar?' I finished my drink. 'Yes,' I said, thinking of Knickers-to-Match and the enraged bee, 'it is very alive with nature. . . .'

All those events took place in 1978 during my initial stay in

Karpathos and when, at George's insistence, I paid a fleeting visit to the island following my return from Kardamena in 1980, I remembered them with affection. But although I spent only twenty-four hours there I found that George was right. In two years there had been changes. The runway on which I landed had been tarmacadamed and in Pigadia a new hotel was being built. At Ammopi which I reached by taxi on a much improved road, Fortula's pension was flourishing and full: it rejoiced in the name 'Hotel Golden Beach'. But friendly hens no longer scratched between the table legs and her taverna. They had been banished. And the old wooden tables had been replaced by ones with formica tops and matching whitewood chairs. They stood within an aluminium extension to the taverna. That had sliding doors, and in the evening it was illuminated by blue strip lighting. Fortula had not changed, but the old atmosphere had gone; and so in the march of progress had two delightful old almirithra trees. I felt a little saddened and said as much to Papadakis before going back to Rhodes. 'It is inevitable,' he said. 'And,' emphasized his son looking up from the proofs of some travel brochures, 'it is business.'

'Yes,' echoed George that evening when I reported back and told him of my reactions, 'it is business.' He chuckled. 'Poor Yanni!' he said, mocking me, 'so many shocks! For your opinion Kardamena now is Sodom, and tomorrow Karpathos will be Gomorrah!' George has a nice turn of phrase in both English and Greek. 'And worse is to come,' he continued, raising his hands in simulated horror and crossing to the drinks cabinet, 'for your last day here we have arranged for you to become a tripper! Yes, Yanni mu,' he said, addressing the glasses and clinking some ice-cubes into them, 'tomorrow we go on a boat excursion –

in *Triton II.*' He added the ouzo. 'Actually,' he said, returning with the tumblers. 'I think you will enjoy it. It's a Finnish block booking. . . .'

Unplanned and unexpectedly, that day decided my movements for the following year.

Triton II was one of a number of pleasure boats engaged in taking tourists on day-trips to the less accessible bays and beaches on the island, and one in which, together with a Swede named Kim, George had a business interest. They were well patronized but as an added inducement, excursionists were plied with free ouzo aboard, given a meal with wine at a beach taverna and offered further libations on the way back. I had on occasions witnessed the return of such jaunts in the late afternoon. They could be, and often were, macabre spectacles.

Among the venues included in the itineraries of these vessels was a bay named in honour of Anthony Quinn. Mr Quinn is remembered by the Greeks for his masculinity and the immortality which he brought to the role of Zorba the Greek. It was a pity, therefore, that the accolade had lost something of its value through the phonetic spelling of the actor's name. 'COME,' I was exhorted by divers placards, and in chalked capitals, 'TO FALIRAKI, KALIMBIA AND TSAMBIKA. *AND*,' they ended, with a triumphant flourish, 'TO ANTHONY QUEEN.' However, and probably because of the mastery of English by its owners, *Triton II* was guiltless of the unintended slur.

Like George, Kim too spoke faultless English. He also spoke Greek and had command of several Scandinavian languages. That morning he was exercising his authority in Finnish. 'Omelette or fish,' he inquired rhythmically from the foot of the gangway as Finn after Finn prepared to embark, 'omelette or fish for your meal at Kalimbia.'

And ticked off their requirements. 'Forty-five omelettes and fifteen fishes,' he advised me as the last one passed him, 'and chips with everything.' He closed the score book with a snap. 'I'll see you later,' he said. 'I'm driving to Kalimbia.' And left to telephone the order.

'Let's go,' said George; and we went aboard.

The Finns were fresh to Rhodes. They were very white, middle-aged and very large, and mostly in need of ironing. They were also very serious. T-shirted and festooned with cameras and unresponsive to the canned bouzoukoi music which played above the throbbing engines, they sat heavily in rows staring at the passing waves through large dark glasses. Solemnly they drank the proffered ouzo and ate the complimentary cheese, gravely they changed into bathing costumes when we stopped at Anthony Queen's, and leadenly they jumped into the sea like obedient lemmings, the more senior of their number clasping their noses as they did so. Nor did further offerings of ouzo serve to unleash them from their inhibitions. They were still constrained when we reached Kalimbia.

'Mana mu,' muttered George fingering his moustache as he watched the first batch of his customers climb sedately into a dinghy and chug towards the shore, 'Michaeli will have to work hard today.' He tapped his teeth. 'You'll meet him shortly,' he said, anticipating my question, 'he's a great character. He'll play his violin and get the people singing with him during lunch.' He paused to look at a quintet of Finns impassively awaiting the return of the boat. 'At least,' he said, 'he'll try to.'

George was correct in every particular. Michaeli was a character. Costumed in black baggy trousers tucked into ankle boots and wearing a silver braided black waistcoat over a blue patterned shirt buttoned at the wrists and with a blue and red scarf about his neck, he waved his fiddle bow in greeting from where he stood with Kim in the taverna and embraced George extravagantly when we met. Hook nosed and heavily moustached with thick grey side whiskers framing a weather worn face from which twinkling dark brown eyes smiled upon the world, Michaeli was a handsome old man. He was also a trier.

For half an hour he moved among the tables, scraping and singing with much panache but in a voice as suspect as his instrument, exhorting the Finns to open their mouths in unison with him. They did so; and filled them with omelette and fish. In Greek he sang to them of love and played 'Viva España' and 'Lilli Marlene'. He even tried 'Auld Lang Syne'. And in a final fling which smacked of desperation, 'She'll Be Coming Round The Mountain When She Comes'. But to no avail. The Finns fed their faces and remained unmoved.

Michaeli returned to our table to a smatter of applause and drained a glass of retsina. Kim looked at him sympathetically and refilled it. 'Try playing the Finnish National Anthem,' he said. 'At least that would make them stand up.' Michaeli smiled ruefully. 'Ah well,' he said philosophically, there's always tomorrow.' 'And,' said George as an immensely fat Finnish lady waddled towards us, 'today is not yet over.'

The flesh mountain wobbled to a halt before Michaeli. 'Plis,' she said, holding a two drachma piece enticingly between her thumb and forefinger, as if encouraging him to sit up and beg, 'plis?' And pursed her lips expectantly.

'I believe,' said George under his breath, 'that she thinks you're a stud. Go on, Michaeli mu! Be brave! Business is business!' Michaeli swallowed hard, closed his eyes, and obliged. 'Epharisto,' he said, and pocketed his fee.

'Bravo,' said Kim as the satisfied one returned to the ranks, 'Greece is proud of you!' He turned to me. 'That's the way it goes,' he said, 'some days are better than others. But I hope you haven't been bored?' 'On the contrary,' I said. 'And I'm glad to have met Michaeli.' Kim nodded. 'He's a fine old man,' he said, and looked affectionately towards him. 'We're old friends. This afternoon I'm taking him to Gennadi. He has some business there.' He stubbed out his cigarette. 'Why not come with us,' he suggested, 'instead of going back on board? We shall only be there for an hour but I think you'll like Gennadi.'

'And so do I,' said George as I accepted the offer and the Finns prepared to depart en masse, 'but I must get back to funland. Yasas!'

It was two o'clock and very hot when the three of us reached Gennadi; and our stay was brief. But although I saw little of the village it took less than an hour for me to fall in love with the place. It had that indefinable aura peculiar to Greek villages, a mixture of timelessness and lack of urgency, a 'take us as you find us' attitude; but above all it had a warmth and an abundance of friendliness, ingredients which soon were made manifest.

'Yasu Yanni,' said Klimi, the owner of the beach taverna to whom Kim had introduced me and with whom he had a rendezvous, 'kalos! kalos! – welcome!'

'What?' called a greybeard from his seat on a bench, 'What's his name?' Yanni,' repeated Klimi. 'Ah!' cried the grizzled one, rising with difficulty to greet me, 'bravo! I'm a Yanni too! Bravo! Bravo! It is a good name. And over there,' he instructed me patting a gnarled hand on my shoulder, 'is another Yanni – he grows cucumbers. And that one with the two teeth,' he continued, pointing to an elderly gentleman in a flat hat and looking remarkably like Bugs Bunny, '*he* is a Yanni! And the one asleep with his mouth open,' concluded my namesake directing my attention to another quarter, 'the one without any teeth, he also is a Yanni – Baba Yanni!' He clapped his hands like an excited child. 'Five Yannis together,' he declared, 'we must have a drink! A bottle, Klimi!' He piloted me towards Bugs Bunny. 'Now where are you from and what do you do, how old are you and are you rich, and how many children have you . . .'

Like Kipling's Elephant's Child the Greek islander has a ''satiable curtiosity'.

That bottle was not the only one to be ingested that afternoon. Each other Yanni pledged another and it was on a wave of euphoria that I was driven back to Rhodes.

'I see,' said George when I presented myself at his flat, and with a touch of envy after his long day with the Finns, 'that you enjoyed Gennadi.' He looked at me searchingly. 'Perhaps you had better sit down,' he said.

I nodded happily. 'I can't wait to go back there,' I said. But I had to wait. For nearly a year.

CHAPTER VII

Yasas, Gennadi

IT WAS MID-SEPTEMBER in 1981 when I was driven south from the tourist cauldron of Rhodes and returned to Gennadi. I stayed there for three idyllic weeks in a little house in the heart of the village. It had considerable charm and, like most traditional dwellings in rural Greece, eccentric plumbing. Within twenty-four hours I discovered that water from a stone sink emptied itself through a pipe placed high in the wall, and thence to the floor of the adjoining outside lavatory. That too, had its own especial problems. However, by the end of a week when I had established that it flushed only on alternate days and was better tempered in the evenings, I adjusted myself to its foibles and we got on famously together.

It was also a great ice-breaker. Each time the cistern clanked and gushed in triumph, our joint victory was applauded by my neighbours, Poppi and Lukas. 'Bravo Yanni!' they would call from their doorstep three yards away across the road; and their small son Yiorgo would run and peer through the metal gate of the tiny courtyard and watch me emerge exultant. It was all very chummy.

Architecturally Gennadi was not particularly attractive. Once planned to be the second town in Rhodes, there was no immediate sign of prosperity. I found a rambling, rundown village, the centre of which was a maze of narrow winding streets and a great many derelict houses with crumbling whitewashed walls, properties which had been allowed to deteriorate by owners who had emigrated to Australia or America. These were happy hunting-grounds for countless rampant Toms who fought and loved and kept their horrid trysts within the roofless shells at night, tormenting the stars with their cries of ecstasy as they made their conquests. But there was little to appeal to human hedonists in Gennadi. Two sleepy cafeneons, a couple of general stores and a brace of beach tavernas more than met the requirements of its three hundred inhabitants who, like the cats, were mostly closely related.

As my impressions of the previous year had led me to believe, they were a simple, friendly community. After my arrival in the early evening, and when I had unpacked and washed and bought some provisions, I walked down to Klimi's taverna on the beach and there I was afforded a welcome similar to the one I received initially. Bugs Bunny and Baba Yanni were present and in excellent fo·m; I met the village vet named Demos, a Christos and a pale blue-eyed Yiorgo, Lukas from across the road; and a nephew of Klimi's called Pavlos who was on holiday from Sydney. He was a spare young man of twenty with long curly hair parted in the middle, steel-rimmed spectacles and spoke both English and Greek with a strong Australian accent. I asked him how long he had been in Gennadi and what had brought him there.

'Blew in about three months ago,' he twanged; and pointed to Klimi's wife Maria who was lying inside on an improvised chaise longue and clutching her stomach. 'That's my Aunty over there,' he disclosed. 'My Mum's sister. Mum married Klimi's brother. Then they buggered off to Australia and had me.' He looked affectionately towards his aunt. 'Poor old bag,' he said, 'She's got the squitters.' He inhaled on a half-smoked cigarette and ejected the smoke noisily in a thin stream. 'Yeah,' he reflected, 'she had 'em when I came and she'll have 'em when I go, I reckon.' He tapped away some ash. 'Nerves,' he diagnosed; 'and too much bloody work; and Klimi's a bastard to her.' He was a likeable youth but like many antipodeans, earthy.

'Been here before?' he asked, laconically. 'Once,' I said, 'just for an hour or so; but I liked it.'

'Yeah,' said Pavlos, 'it's beaut. Just like the folks told me back home.' He took a last draw at the stub of his cigarette, holding it close to his lips between his thumb and forefinger. 'An' you know something, Jono?' he said interrogatively and screwing the butt-end into a tin ashtray, 'I feel just right here.' He tamped out the last of the sparks. 'My word I do.'

'Oriste?' said Yanni Bugs Bunny on behalf of the rest of the company, feeling that they had been left in the cold too long, 'what are you saying?' Pavlos translated the conversation. 'But of course you feel at home,' they chorused, 'you *are* Greek!'

'Too right,' said Pavlos in Australian, 'too bloody right!' He laughed. 'You know I've only spoken English twice since I came here.' He laughed again. 'Oh my word,' he said; and nodded in the direction of a deeply tanned but sad-looking girl who was sitting forlornly at a table and gazing into an empty glass. 'See that sheila,' he asked, 'the one with the charlies?' 'Yes,' I said, appreciatively, 'I do.'

'Too right,' said Pavlos. 'She's Canadian. And two days ago you'd have seen a bit more of her mate. Oh my word, you would!' He broke off to enlighten the Yannis. 'Ah yes,' they agreed, their age dropping from them like Autumn leaves, 'you would have. Much more!' 'Anyway,' continued Pavlos, 'there she was, lying on the beach over there with her bloke. She had her whatsit covered, but he didn't. Harry Starkers he was. I ask you!' said Pavlos. 'Right in front of the taverna, the stupid bastard!' Again he brought the others into the picture. 'Yes,' they concurred, 'very stupid. And rude.'

'Anyhow,' pursued Pavlos, 'Old Katrina, who works in the kitchen, saw them. She screamed her head off and got hold of the police, they got hold of the bods, took 'em up to the station, nobody understood anybody so they brought me in as interpreter. And that,' said he, lighting a fresh cigarette, 'is why she's by herself. They let her go, but they've taken the bloke to Rhodes. He goes to court tomorrow and she's been crying her bloody eyes out ever since, poor bitch. But like I said to her in the station,' concluded Pavlos, 'boobs is O.K., but you must cover your organisms.'

'Exactly!' said Yanni Bugs Bunny after another translation.

'Precisely!' endorsed Baba Yanni, 'the organs must be covered.'

Pavlos looked appraisingly at the bereft one through his cigarette smoke and half-closed his eyes. 'Mind you,' he said, 'if that bloke goes inside for a few days, I wouldn't mind taking over. She's got beaut grapefruits . . . .'

It was an illuminating introduction to the social life of Gennadi and it gave me an insight into the moral yardstick of the village. Also, as the night wore on I was given an ample demonstration of the Gennadians' general ability to dispatch retsina and of that of Yanni Bugs Bunny in particular. The tutorial was lengthy and thorough and midnight had been passed when, with the two Yannis and a bottle, I was driven back to the house by Lukas in his three-wheeler truck. This he parked uncertainly on a small adjacent patch of waste ground, and then with even less certainty, joined us in the courtyard.

He was a well built, unkempt man in his early forties whose face and unruly mop of hair were permanently decorated with flecks of dried emulsion paint and plaster as a reminder of his daytime occupation. In the evenings he worked at Klimi's. Intellectually he was not very gifted and spent much of his time staring vacantly into space with his mouth wide open. He laughed easily and frequently, and very loudly; and he too enjoyed his retsina.

Half an hour later we bade each other goodnight. The two Yannis departed happily but in good order to their nearby homes, and Lukas, equally content but with less control, crossed the road to his gate. With difficulty he jerked it open and teetering forward, allowed himself to be carried by its momentum. Involuntarily halting at the end of its swing, he paused, rocked back on his heels, remained upon them and then, backpedalling swiftly and still clasping the gate, pulled it after him. It shut with a clang dislodging his hold as it did so and deposited him unceremoniously in the street.

'Then barazi,' he slurred as he staggered to his feet; and brayed into the night.

His second attempt, although no less noisy, was successful. 'Kalinichta,' he whispered hoarsely and indistinctly from the other side of the gate; and slowly waved to me through the open metalwork. 'Kalinichta,' I whispered back; and watched him approach the door of the house. That too presented him with a challenge; and that also was closed with a bang. Seconds later there was the noise of assorted pots and pans clattering to the floor followed, after the briefest of pauses, by the wailing of a child and Poppi's voice raised stridently in fury and inquiry.

Like her husband, Poppi was not an intellectual but her eloquence surprised me – as did the power of her lungs. Addressing him for several minutes in the key of E, and with very few pauses, most of her remarks concerned the lateness of the hour and his condition, but she also included several references to his other shortcomings. These appeared to be legion and remarkably varied. The harangue ended with the sound of breaking pottery, the slamming of another door and then, silence.

I felt quite sorry for Lukas.

The next morning I awoke early to find an elderly hen looking down its beak at me from the foot of my bed. For a split second we eyed each other in mutual disbelief then, as I reacted to its presence, it picked up its skirts and fled through the open door clucking hysterically as it went. It was a rude awakening.

I got out of bed, picked up a feather it had shed in its panic, and collected my soap and towel. Remembering the quirks of the sink, I elected to wash at a standpipe to the left of the courtyard gate. That was still ajar and through the gap I could see Poppi already ensconced on her doorstep with her legs stretched into the roadway and engrossed with some sewing.

'Kalimera!' she screeched as the sound of splashing reached her and the water started to trickle down the steps and into the road, 'ti kanete?'

We eyed each other in mutual disbelief.

'Kala!' I shouted over the wall, 'and you?' 'Aach!' she rasped back, 'that Lukas! He slept in the kitchen last night! You understand? In the kitchen! I made him sleep in the kitchen! On the floor! And this morning he had a bad headache!' She laughed triumphantly and hoarsely but without rancour; and changed the subject. 'What will you do today?' 'I shall walk,' I called out, towelling my face, 'but now I shall have some breakfast.' I turned off the tap. 'See you later,' I said; and went inside to make some coffee.

Five minutes later Poppi appeared in the doorway with little Yiorgo and a ten year old girl with buck teeth. She was wearing a T-shirt emblazoned 'Disco Queen' and clasping a bunch of basil. 'Parakalo,' she said shyly; and presented it to me.

'My niece Maria,' said Poppi who was carrying a large plateful of water melon and some black figs, 'her mother is my sister who is married to the brother of Christos who you met last night in Klimi's. Do you like kapoozi?' 'Very much,' I said, 'and figs.' 'Endaxi,' said Poppi, 'kali orexi!' She was a squat little thing with coarse black hair and pock-marked skin, but it was not until she limped back to her house with the children that I realized that she had a club foot. But her eyes were brown and beautiful, and her face was soft and kind.

'Epharisto para poli,' I said when later I returned the plate at the start of my walk. 'Tipota,' said Poppi, and wished me well.

'Kalimera!' croaked three old ladies dressed in black as I approached them at the end of the street, 'you were late back last night with Lukas! He slept in the kitchen you know! And he broke a pot! Po! Po! Po!' I left them huddled together and clacking happily and turned the corner reflecting on the efficiency of the bush telegraph system of the village. I wondered if they knew about the hen.

I made my way through the complex of streets, exchanging greetings as I went until, with the nucleus of the village behind me, I reached the sloping tree-lined avenue which led to Klimi's taverna and intercepted the coastal road to Rhodes. I crossed it, passed by a rusting wreck of a Chevrolet saloon now serving as a home for hens, and picked my way diagonally downhill along a winding rocky path. To one side of it were scattered tumbledown outhouses and on the other, a high-banked field with overhanging fig trees giving shade to tethered goats and donkeys. The air was acrid with their smell.

A few yards ahead of me two figures appeared from around a bend in the track. One was a wizened, black-draped old woman seated on an overladen donkey, and plodding in her wake and bent double under a bundle of faggots and dragging a huge piece of whitened driftwood, came another lady of similar vintage and attire. All three looked very weary.

'Yasu!' cried the rider kicking her heels into the donkey's side and belabouring its rump with a stick but with no measurable result, 'Kalos! Kalos!'

'Yasu!' echoed her companion as the distance between us closed, and dropped her load at my feet. 'Po! Po! Po!' she gasped, drawing a muscular arm across her forehead, 'it is very hot, ne?' She was a fat, brawny woman and appeared considerably stronger than the donkey.

'Ne,' I agreed, 'it is hot. Can I help you?' She looked affronted as if I was doubting her fitness. 'Oche!' she said, tossing her head back, 'it is not far.' She pointed to the top of the hill. 'Just there,' she said. 'But where are you going?' I shrugged my shoulders, 'I don't know,' I said, 'I only arrived yesterday.' 'Ne!' squeaked the wizened one, 'we know! we know! Your name is Yanni and you come from England and last night you were in Klimi's!'

'Yes,' endorsed Fatso, 'with Yanni and Pavlos and Lukas and Christos! And you drank much retsina!' 'Poli!' cackled her friend throwing up her hands and all but unseating herself, 'and so did Lukas! Too much! He slept in the kitchen and smashed all the crockery! We know – Christos told us when we were picking figs. His brother is married to the sister of Lukas's wife. That is how we know.' 'Yes,' mimicked Fatso, 'that is how we know!' And drawing back their thin lips they laughed loudly and toothlessly in unison.

Once again I marvelled at Gennardi's intelligence network. If not accurate in every particular it was remarkable for its speed.

'And what are your names?' I asked.

'Anthi,' lisped Fatso covering me with a fine spray.

'Thespe,' sibilated the other with equal difficulty, and dipped into a pannier. 'Have some figs,' she said, producing a double handful. 'Ne,' said Anthi doing likewise, 'and here is a bag. There!' she said, emptying the weeping green fruit into it, 'and now – andio!' With one hand she hoisted her bundle on to her back, and grasping the rope attached to the log, slung it over her left shoulder and took the strain. 'Endaxi?' she inquired of Thespe. 'Endaxi,' said Thespe fetching her mount a resounding thwack, and off they went discussing me in high-pitched voices.

That was the first of many encounters I was to have with Anthi and Thespe. Each day I would meet them, either at the start of my walk early in the morning as they returned from their fig harvesting, or find them on my way back, sitting together on their doorsteps, cracking piles of almonds with outsize hammers.

'Ella!' they would call, 'come and sit down and tell us your news!' And I would join them and gossip for a while and leave with my mouth sticky with the syrup of sugar-saturated apricots. Nor did I ever go empty handed. Figs, black and green, almonds and olives, all were pressed upon me daily despite my protestations at the generosity. 'Oche!' they said, raising their hands, 'it is nothing! Would you not do the same for us if we came to your country?'

I have often recalled the remark, and felt ashamed; for even in the smallest English hamlet I doubt if the Anthis and Thespes of this world would be shown such simple warmth, so quickly. And it was that, and similar thoughts which occupied me as I watched them move slowly up the hill on that first morning and then went on my way, clasping my bag of figs.

Close before me and black and shiny in the heat, lay the main road which ran from Rhodes to the small town of Katavia in the south-west of the island. I reached it, and with the sea on my left, blue gorse-covered hills to my right and flanked on both sides by ditches and lower lying olive groves bordered by fig and almond trees, I set off along it.

A strong breeze from the hills fluttered the voluminous skirts of women working in the fields and caught at the loose polythene sheeting of plastic greenhouses making them flap and crack like the lash of stock whips; but it kept down the heat and walking was pleasant.

Only one vehicle passed me within the first ten minutes. It was a pick-up truck. Driven with unusual care by Greek standards and travelling slowly, it contained a brown and white pointer dog, a heap of kapoozi upon which was seated a very small lady; and the village priest. Standing erect and grasping the back of the cab with both hands and with the wind catching at his robes and blowing through his beard, he stared resolutely ahead like Moses in sight of the Promised Land.

Two hundred yards further on, the truck came to a halt beside a building enclosed by a long white wall. Upon it, and crudely daubed in red paint, was the hammer and sickle, and in large capitals the initials, K.K.E.

The driver got out, walked slowly to the rear of the truck, unlatched the tail-board and assisted his passengers down. Then, presenting the lady with a monstrous kapoozi under the weight of which she plainly wilted, he crossed himself twice and drove away. The papas disappeared behind the wall followed closely and bow-legged by the kapoozi-laden lady.

As I had deduced, the building was a chapel. Like the outer wall it was similarly disfigured with graffiti. It lay well back from the road behind a small courtyard with a central fig tree around which was built a circular wooden seat. Upon it rested the giant kapoozi.

To the left was a small whitewashed building. That too had received attention. Curiosity led me to make a closer examination of the handiwork and I walked across to it. Whoever had executed it had scorned an aerosol and used oil paint and an overloaded brush.

K.K.E. The letters dripped red. I stood looking at them lost in thought as I teased the tobacco in my pouch and filled my pipe.

'Ine kakos, ne?' crackled a voice from behind me, making me jump; and turning around I came face to face with the papas. Like all priests of the Greek Orthodox

Church his face was all but hidden under a full bushy beard making his age difficult to determine but I judged him to be nearer seventy than sixty. And like all Greek country clergy his general appearance suggested that of a stage magician at the close of a long provincial tour. He was very dusty and, as the shoulders of his black robes betrayed, suffered badly from dandruff.

'It is bad, yes?' he repeated. 'Yes,' I said, 'very bad'. He stretched out a hand lumpy with arthritis and rubbed his fingers against the lettering as if trying to erase it. 'Kappa Kappa Epsilon,' he said, 'Communiste! Askimos – the Ugly Ones!' 'I know,' I said, 'but where do they come from?'

He shrugged. 'I don't know,' he said. 'Maybe from Crete, but not from here. But they are very wicked and against God. They have broken into many churches and slashed the icons with big knives and done many other terrible things.' He pointed towards the hills. 'Such blasphemies they have committed at the monastery at Skiathe,' he said; 'and even when we lock the doors they break them in, these Antichrists.' He shook his head sadly and changed the subject. 'Do you like Gennadi? he asked. I nodded. 'Ne,' he said, 'it is a good village. You are staying near my house. My wife saw you buying bread and yoghourt yesterday. Also some cheese, she said; and two mosquito coils.' I made a mental note of the accuracy of the inventory.

As he spoke his tiny informant emerged from the chapel door, shut and locked it and peered myopically at us through thick-lensed spectacles. 'Ah!' she exclaimed as we swam into her vision; and scurried towards us carrying a handful of half-used candles. Dressed from head to foot in dark brown even to her thick stockings and unencumbered by the kapoozi she moved quickly like a snub-nosed mole.

'My wife,' said the papas punctiliously but unnecessarily as she reached us; and we exchanged greetings. Once again I was obliged to disclose my curriculum vitae including my denomination, the frequency of my attendances at public worship in England, the value of the gold crucifix about my neck, and the length of my intended stay in Gennadi. Pleased that I was an Anglican and surprised to learn that I actually went to church, they invited me to join them that very evening at the little chapel of Aghia Anastasia on the other side of the village. It was, so Mrs Papas advised me as she gave me directions how to reach it, very old and very beautiful; and the papas would be saying his offices there at five o'clock. And so saying she passed the candles to her husband, flitted across to the circular seat and grasping the kapoozi with both hands adopted once more the stance of a shrunken cello player and staggered with it towards the road. There she set it down and within seconds and after a spirited if reckless display of callisthenics in the face of an oncoming and fast moving lorry they obtained a lift back to Gennadi, on this occasion travelling cabin class.

I waved goodbye to them as they departed in a cloud of diesel fumes and continued on my way in the opposite direction cogitating as I did so how strange it was that neither had referred to Lukas's fall from grace. Even allowing for the fact that the papas's left ear was decorated with an outmoded hearing aid I found it hard to believe that news of the lapse had failed to reach him. After much consideration I concluded that the omission of reference was due to his obedience to the cloth rather than poor reception.

I walked for another two miles, passed only occasionally

by light traffic, meeting no one and preceded by a pair of pied wagtails. Swooping low over the ground in an undulating flight and landing ahead of me, they twinkled across the road on delicate legs, darting this way and that with beaks agape in their pursuit of flying insects. Then, with their catch accomplished they would dash towards me, and with nodding heads and bobbing tails, halt, take off again with a high pitched 'tschizz' and repeat the procedure as if urging me onwards. They were delightful little creatures and I was saddened when I came upon the body of one by the roadside. Only recently killed by a passing car it was still warm to the touch when I picked it up and the bloom was still on its feathers.

I lobbed it in a gentle arc into the field below and walked on until I came to the concrete shoulders of a bridge spanning a dried-up river. I paused to look over its side, then leaving the road I clambered down the steep rocky bank which led to the river bed beset with bulrush and rhododendron bushes and slowly followed its course.

There was no breeze below the level of the stubble-fields and the air was oppressive and humid. It wrapped around me like a warm damp blanket and I felt the sweat begin to run down the nape of my neck and soak into my collar. From high above me on the left bank came the deep murmur of a million bees as they swarmed in an almirithra tree. Its foliage shimmered in a brown haze under the weight of their numbers and there was a menace in their sound which accentuated the feeling of airlessness. But where I stood, not a leaf stirred. The only movements were those of dragonflies which, dressed in reds and greens and electric blues, hovered uncertainly on gossamer wings above the sun-baked flaking mud.

Circumspectly I made my way towards the river mouth

and the sea, hopscotching from stone to stone as the surface became boggy and skirting small pools green with algae and alive with frogs. Then, as the ground fell away on either side and the rushes thinned and silt gave way to sand, I felt the breeze again as I reached the open beach.

Before me, a stretch of powdery sand, spiked with tussocks and tall white aromatic lilies and untidy with flotsam and goat-droppings, sloped down to a deserted shingled shore pebbled with greens and reds. And there, comfortable with the knowledge that I would offend no one, I stripped off my clothes and plunged into a warm and very salt sea.

For half an hour I swam in it, peering through the crystal-clear water at shoals of tiny fish weaving and darting with massed precision between gently waving weeds, and then, with my hands cupped behind my head, I stretched out upon my back on the smooth shingle. High overhead an osprey effortlessly spiralled on a thermal, and from somewhere in the distant hills behind me came the faint tinkling of goat bells as a herd was driven to another grazing. And I felt as free as the wind which brought the music to me.

It was early afternoon when I returned to the house and to a deserted street. Gennadi was having its siesta and for the next two hours I followed suit before setting out to keep my appointment with the papas.

'Yasu Yanni!' called Poppi from her doorstep as I opened my gate, 'did you have a good day? We have heard that you met the papas, ne?' 'Yes,' I said, 'I did.' 'Ah yes,' said Lukas who was sitting next to her, 'the priest.' He stopped picking his nose and crossed himself. 'I am good friends with the papas,' he volunteered – 'only this morning I gave him ten drachmas for the church.' 'Ne,' said Poppi, 'to make a special prayer for you. For forgiveness,' she added archly. And stuck her elbow in his stomach. 'Huh! Huh!' said Lukas; and looked more than ever like the Fool in King Lear. In view of the certainty that his extravagances of the previous night had not been his first and were unlikely to be his last, I wondered if he had considered making a standing order.

CHAPTER VIII

Bad Dogs and Worse Imaginings

IT WAS A PRETTY walk to the little chapel of Aghia
Anastasia. Obeying the papas's directions and leaving
Poppi and Lukas still engaged in low-comedy badinage,
I walked to the top of the street, paused to look down over
an open coastal plain and then rounded a bend beneath the
walls of Gennadi's church. There the road stopped
abruptly and, as I had been instructed, I took to a steeply
winding downhill footpath which cut deeply through
terraced allotments thick with citrus and pomegranate
trees. Their leafy branches met overhead in a low green
canopy through which the sunlight flickered, and on either
side of me water from a hidden spring bubbled down
concrete irrigation channels and leaked across the path
through cracks in their sides. Verdant and cool, it was a
fairyland tunnel from which I emerged at the foot of
Gennadi's hills. And there, in the open ground and
enclosed by the low white walls of a graveyard and
approached on my right by a cypress-lined avenue, was
the tiny chapel. Windowless and squat, it could have been
a plaster of Paris decoration taken from a Christmas cake.

The rusty gate of the cemetery squealed as I unlatched it and disturbed a widow kneeling at a graveside. She looked up and nodded to me as I made my way through an arched portico to the half-opened chapel door beyond. From within came the smell of incense and the murmur of the papas's voice as he said his offices. Gently I pushed the door further ajar and entered quietly. No sunlight had ever touched the inner walls and I felt the chill of centuries; and shivered.

For a moment I stood still, letting my eyes adjust to the dimly lit interior illuminated only by four oil-lamps suspended from the chapel roof in ornate brass baskets. Below the farthest from me, and perched precariously upon a step-ladder, was the papas's wife. In one hand she held a bottle of oil and in the other, a rag. Of her husband there was no sign, but his voice reached me as he intoned from somewhere in the shadows.

'Amin,' said his wife in response to his orison before a hidden icon; and topped up the lamp and wiped it clean. 'Amin,' came the voice from the darkness.

I moved towards a row of wooden stalls to the left of the chapel and sat in one of them, my arms resting on the well-worn high supports; and for a few seconds I closed my eyes and bowed my head to our mutual God. When I opened them the details of the chapel were clearer.

On the wall on my right I saw a huge, magnificent though crude, unjaded fresco depicting the story of Jonah being swallowed by the whale. Unfaded by strong light, the colours were as fresh as the day they had been applied by the loving hands of the artist seven hundred and fifty years before. Facing me was another line of high backed stalls of olive-wood, their arms polished and gleaming with the patina of ages. Gracing the wall behind them were innumerable icons of bygone saints. And suddenly, in that little roughcast whitewashed chantry in a village of no importance, I was brought face to face with the simple faith of simple people. The Cross of Calvary I thought, was still more potent than the Hammer and Sickle.

'Amin,' said Mrs Papas responding again to another invocation; and came down the ladder. 'It's stopped smoking,' she said; and scuttled into the dimness.

'Good,' said her husband, appearing from the gloom and stopping to kiss an icon, 'Amin.' 'It was the wick,' said his wife, reappearing with a feather duster and putting it to use as he made a fresh veneration, 'Amin.' 'Amin,' said the papas, swinging his censer in my direction and blessing me in a cloud of incense, 'Amin'; and continued his tour of the icons with his wife in close attendance. There was no doubting their sincerity but as I slipped out I wondered if ever again I would witness a combined spring-cleaning and prayer session.

I did not return to the village by the papas's short-cut. Instead, I walked out of the cemetery gates and followed the long straight concrete road between the lines of cypress trees. The early evening was very still and the air was strident with the trilling of cicadas as they sang between the branches.

A very old lady, bent double with arthritis and dressed in widow's weeds, hobbled slowly and painfully in my direction, her face towards the ground. She was holding a small bunch of flowers in either hand and singing quietly to herself as she advanced, oblivious of my approach. I called out good evening as I neared her, and she stopped. Two red-rimmed, watery blue eyes, opaque with extreme age and set in a shrivelled face focused falteringly upon me. 'Kalos,' she piped; and repeated the greeting.

The eyes wavered, turned uncertainly to the flowers and then back to me. 'Are they not beautiful?' she asked, as a child would do; and slowly raised them to my nose. Obligingly I sniffed at the posies. 'They are most beautiful,' I said, 'and their perfume is lovely.' 'Ne,' she said, 'it is a good smell. They are for my husband.' With difficulty she motioned towards the cemetery. 'He is asleep up there,' she said; 'by the wall.' For a moment she gazed unseeingly into the distance, lost in a private world, then slowly turned to me again. 'Soon I shall sleep there too,' she said, 'quite soon you understand.' She smiled wearily but happily. 'And that will be good,' she said. 'We shall be together. With God.' She nodded reassuringly to herself. 'Ne,' she repeated, 'with God.' She looked once more into nirvana and then bidding me goodbye, went singing reedily upon her way.

When I reached the end of the avenue I turned and looked back along it to the graveyard gates to which it led. It was, I thought, the perfect pathway to one's journey's end.

I turned and began to trudge along the dusty uphill road which would take me back into the village. To my left the ground sloped steeply away in neglected terraces towards the coast. Below me, close to the roadside and in the shade of fruitless banana trees, turkeys gobbled and wobbled their livid wattles in wire-netted pens – ugly birds, disgruntled and quarrelsome and angry with the world from the time they leave the egg. I have never felt kindly towards them, and crossed to the other side. That was abutted by a small grove of ripening orange and lemon trees enclosed by chain-linked fencing which ran down from an imposing two-storeyed building at the top of the hill. This, as I discovered when I drew abreast of it, was the police station to which the hapless naked ones had been escorted some days before. And it was down its steps that Klimi limped.

Looking neither to the right nor to the left and disregarding my salutation, angrily he mounted his moped and drove away. Hitherto a friendly little man, I wondered what had caused his churlishness, and his disability. I also reflected that it should not be long before I was edified.

'Yasu Yanni,' called Poppi who was still in situ when I reached my gate and who was cognizant of where I had been, 'were you blessed?' 'I was,' I said. 'And the paintings on the wall,' she asked, 'were they not wonderful?' I agreed. 'And is it not amazing,' she continued, 'that such a man could live in such a belly and then be sicked up? Whole?' 'Truly amazing,' I said; and went in to have a wash.

Fifteen minutes later, freshened and dressed in slacks, I shut the gate behind me and began my walk to Klimi's taverna. I did not get far.

'Yanni!' called Baba Yanni as I came to the first of the village's two cafeneons, 'ella mu!' And beckoned me over. I did as I was bidden.

'Sit down! Sit down!' commanded Baba Yanni who was not dissimilar to a pipeless Popeye in a flat hat; and gestured towards a cadaverous old gentleman with sunken eyes who was sitting with him. 'Panayotis,' he disclosed as he introduced us, 'my elder daughter's godfather.' 'Yasu!' said Panayotis, shaking hands with me, 'what will you drink – ouzo or retsina?' I opted for the former. 'Bravo!' said Panayotis pressing down upon the table top and levering himself on to infirm feet, 'it is good for the stomach.' He placed his hand gently upon his own. 'I suffer from my stomach,' he said. 'Greatly. Each day I drink a glass of ouzo to comfort it. Sometimes two.' 'Or three,' said Baba Yanni.' 'Ne,' agreed Panayotis, 'or even four. It depends on the stomach, you understand;' and went inside to declare his wishes. From his gait I surmised that it had been a bad day for stomachs.

'Stinyamas!' said Baba Yanni when the order arrived in company with some olives and fetta; and we clinked our glasses together and embarked upon the Greeks' favourite pastime. Conversation.

Baba Yanni did not ask me how I had passed the hours since he and Yanni Bugs Bunny had left me the previous night. He told me. Accurately. In every particular. Predictably Lukas received a mention in dispatches. 'But now,' said Baba Yanni interrogatively when he had finished his résumé of my activities and patting me on my knee, 'what will you do?' He beamed toothlessly at me and awaited a preview of my plans for the evening. 'I shall go for a meal,' I said; 'at Klimi's.'

'Ah!' said Baba Yanni taking a sip at his ouzo, 'Klimi!'

'Ah!' said Panayotis doing likewise, 'Klimi!'

'Do you know about Klimi?' asked Baba Yanni spearing a piece of fetta and force feeding me from the end of the fork, 'do you know what happened to him today?'

'Oche,' I said through the cheese, 'but I saw him coming from the police station. I think he had hurt his foot.'

'Ne,' said Baba Yanni, 'he had. He was bitten by a dog.'

'Badly,' confirmed Panayotis, 'by a black dog.'

'With a white spot,' added Baba Yanni ever mindful of detail, 'the dog of the Kosta of the other cafeneon, who smokes the pipe. It rushed out upon him as he went past on his motor cycle –'

'Barking fiercely,' Panayotis reminded him. 'Ne,'

acknowledged Baba Yanni, 'barking fiercely; and snarling. It –'

'Seized him by the ankle!' interrupted Panayotis biting his wrist and worrying it between his gums.

'Tore him from his machine!' continued Baba Yanni entering into the pantomime and pulling Panayotis towards him.

'Went for his throat!' cried Panayotis accepting the challenge and clawing at his neck.

'Tried to savage him!' shouted Baba Yanni, working his jaw furiously and going for an Oscar.

'But was pulled away just in time,' said Panayotis, competitive to the end and sending the olives flying. 'Ne,' said Baba Yanni, nearly spent but determined to have the curtain line, '*just* in time!' And drained his ouzo.

Equally debilitated Panayotis followed suit and then refilled his glass. 'But when,' I asked, 'did all this happen? When did you see it?' 'Parakalo?' said Baba Yanni. I repeated the question. 'Ah,' said Baba Yanni, 'we did not actually *see* it. But Christos who is married to my elder daughter he saw the attack and told her of it. And she told her mother who informed the wife of Panayotis; and he told me. That is so, ne?' he asked of his friend. 'Sosta,' said Panayotis once more addressing himself to his ouzo. 'And so,' said Baba Yanni, 'that is how we know it to be true.'

I looked at Panayotis who seemed to be having difficulty in finding the rim of his glass. 'Yes,' I said, 'I see,' and changed the subject. 'Will you be coming to Klimi's later?'

'Oche,' said Baba Yanni. 'Soon I shall go to bed because tomorrow I shall be up early. Very early,' he emphasized, 'hunting. With Christos. Tomorrow the hunting season begins you understand.' 'Ne,' said Panayotis pointing an imaginary rifle unsteadily towards the roofing, 'bam! bam!' 'And will you be hunting?' I asked him. He peered dyspeptically into his empty glass as if to find the answer in its dregs. 'Perhaps,' he said; 'but it will depend on my stomach.' 'Perhaps,' I suggested, 'another ouzo will soothe it – ne?' 'Ne,' said Panayotis after the briefest consideration, 'why not? Epharisto.'

His gastric disorders were still under discussion when I left but I hoped that for everyone's safety he would remain abed in ‚the morning. His trigger finger was distinctly shaky.

The taverna was not a hive of industry when I reached it. The well-endowed survivor of the police enquiry, still without her brazen partner, was sitting happily with Pavlos who, to judge from the position of his hands, appeared to have gained her complete confidence; Lukas, continuing to be occupied with nasal exploration but otherwise unemployed, was leaning against the wall; Demos the Vet was playing backgammon with the local doctor; inside, Klimi's wife had her feet up and was watching a television quiz programme; and Christos, Yanni Bugs Bunny and the pale-eyed Yiorgo were sitting together by the doorway half listening to bouzoukoi music from a tape recorder.

'Where's Klimi?' I asked as I went over to them. 'Inside,' said Christos, 'standing on one leg.' 'Ne,' said Bugs Bunny, 'like a stork.' 'Also,' said Christos, 'his mood is not good. He was bitten –'

'I know,' I said, 'by a dog. Baba Yanni told me.' 'Oh!' said Christos, clearly put out that he had been scooped by his father-in-law, 'well go and see his leg and then come back.' 'That's right,' said Yanni encouragingly, 'go and see his leg – he may not have it tomorrow.'

For a man whom I had been given to understand had been all but mauled to death and rolled in the dust to boot, Klimi had made a remarkable recovery; but he was certainly still taciturn. I listened patiently to his account of the incident, looked sympathetically at the barely broken skin, agreed that both the dog and its owner should be shot without delay, ordered a meal; and returned to the table with a couple of bottles.

'What are you going to eat?' inquired Bugs Bunny as he poured the retsina. 'Octopus,' I said; 'and salad,' I added as Lukas brought the latter to the table. 'Ah,' exclaimed Christos, following the example of the others and raising his glass to me, 'but tomorrow you shall have meat!' 'Ne,' said Bugs Bunny annexing a slice of onion from my plate with his finger and thumb, 'perhaps partridge! Or even hare!' 'Or rabbit,' said Christos, 'or maybe pigeon. For tomorrow you understand, we go bam! bam!' 'Sosta!' said Bugs Bunny – 'bam-bam! bam-bam!' 'Of course!' I said, 'tomorrow you hunt! Good luck to you all!' And once again we raised our glasses and drank to their hoped for successes. All but Yiorgo.

Plump and fortyish he wore a permanent smile on a kind fat face, but there was no humour in it; and the eyes which were of the palest blue could have been made of glass. But his voice was soft. 'I shall not be hunting tomorrow,' he announced. 'You see, I was bereaved today. Quite suddenly you understand. In Rhodes. This very morning.' And he smiled at us all in turn.

Strangely he did not give me the impression of a man who had recently suffered a severe personal loss. Also, I found it singular that apart from exchanging glances, neither Christos nor Yanni reacted to his sad news; but I said I was sorry and offered him my condolences.

And he smiled at us all in turn.

'Yes,' said Yiorgo, taking a sip of retsina and addressing no one in particular as my octopus arrived, 'it was very tragic. My cousin,' he revealed. 'He was crossing the road you understand. A taxi came from one way, a lorry from the other and they met with him in the middle.' He shook his head. 'It was very unfortunate. Yes,' he continued, 'quite disastrous. His arms came off, his legs came off and his head came off – one after the other.' He shook his head again and reached for his glass. 'And besides,' he said, taking another sip, 'he was so tired.'

'What a pity,' said Christos; helping himself to a portion of tentacle. 'Yes' said Bugs Bunny, 'a great blow;' and deliberately knocked my tobacco pouch to the ground. 'Sighnomi,' he said, and tweaking my trouser leg stuck his head under the table. I took the hint and joined him below. 'Take no notice,' he said in a stage whisper, and screwed his finger against his temple. 'This happens. It is perhaps the moon. Last month it was his uncle. He was burned to death in Macedonia. In April his brother was drowned off Crete – the God knows who it will be next. Or where. But he will be all right tomorrow. Katalavis Yanni?' 'Katalava,' I said, and retrieved my pouch.

'And so,' said Christos as we surfaced together and I began to make inroads into my octopus, 'as I was saying to Yiorgo, I shall go soon to my house.' He stretched his arms and yawned. 'Hypnos,' he said, putting his palms together and laying his cheek on them, 'also I have to check my guns.' 'Ne,' said Bugs Bunny – 'bam! bam!' Christos stood up. 'Kalinichta si olus,' he said, and went inside to pay his bill. Not long after his departure Yanni followed in his footsteps and I was left with Yiorgo.

'You have eaten very little,' he said, as I mopped up the remains of my octopus and salad with a hunk of bread.

'And you have had nothing,' I told him. 'Oche,' he said, 'my meal is in my house. It is fish. It was cooking when I left.' He paused as a thought occurred to him. 'Perhaps,' he asked, 'you would like to eat some with me? Also we could drink some retsina. Or raki?' He looked at me unblinkingly, still smiling. 'Please,' he said, 'it will help me forget my bereavement.'

Behind me there was a snap as Demos and the doctor closed their backgammon board, startling Lukas who had been dozing at a table with his head in his arms. Of Pavlos and his partner there was no sign, and inside I could see Klimi strumming ill-temperedly on his counter, willing us to go. I thought hard for a moment. 'Epharisto,' I said, 'you are most kind. I should like very much to come to your house.'

'Poso?' I asked Klimi, when I went in to settle my account. 'Tipota,' he said. 'Christos paid for your meal and Yanni for the retsina. Kalinichta.'

Yiorgo's house was a five minute walk from the taverna. Fronted by an untidy plot of ground decorated with the remains of a tractor and divers other pieces of agricultural machinery which showed up clearly in the light of a waning moon, it lay back from the uphill road to the village. Like most of the dwellings in Gennardi it was single-storeyed and possessed a small walled courtyard with a metal gate. Yiorgo's was tied shut with a length of cord. As he unloosed the bow a bright meteor streaked across the sky, glowing red as it vaporized. 'Ah!' exclaimed Yiorgo, 'a shooting star! That means a death somewhere.' 'Or a birth,' I suggested, entering the realm of universal folklore. 'Oche!' insisted Yiorgo, 'it is always a death.' And led the way to the house. I tried hard to think of how I could divert his thoughts from shrouds and sepulchres and prayed for inspiration; but it was fate that intervened. From an outside kitchen came a strong smell of burnt fish.

'My God!' said Yiorgo, rushing to the door and flinging it open, 'my gropas!' And switching on the light he disappeared into a pall of smoke. He emerged hastily from the core of it coughing and spluttering and carrying a smoking pan. Quickly he put it on the ground. 'I am afraid,' he said with masterly understatement as he looked at the incinerated remains below, 'that they have overcooked.'

He tut-tutted. 'This would not have happened if my wife had been here,' he allowed, 'but she is in Katavia you understand.' For a moment he gazed dejectedly at the funeral pyre as if considering suttee, and then pulled himself together. 'Thenbarazi,' he said, 'there is plenty of cheese;' and guided me briskly into the house.

'Ella Yanni,' he said as we entered the living room, and taking me gently by the elbow escorted me swiftly into another containing a double bed and an outsize television set standing on a table. 'Ne,' he said approvingly, 'this is better I think. We can sit on the bed together and eat cheese. Endaxi Yanni?' 'Endaxi,' I said. 'Malista,' smiled Yiorgo, and gave a little bow. He reminded me of a puppy, eager and anxious to please.

We did sit on the bed together, and we did eat cheese. Extremely old cheese. It had a fine green fur and was as hard as nails; and so was the bread which was also coated. And we did watch television. For an hour. It was Huxley's *Brave New World*; with Greek sub-titles. And as the Gammas smiled contentedly from the screen so Yiorgo smiled back at them, fixedly and uncomprehendingly; and drinking steadily.

It was eleven o'clock when he fell asleep and gently slipped sideways on to his bed, clasping an empty glass. He did not stir when I eased it from his grasp and lifted his legs on to the bed. And when I tiptoed from the room, he was still smiling. And so were the Gammas.

I met no one on my way back to the house. Gennardi slept and only the moon showed urgency as it sailed across a clouding sky. Nor was there any activity in Lukas's ménage. For a while I sat outside in the courtyard smoking a last pipe and reliving the events of the day as the moths fluttered around the bracket lamp. From somewhere in the village a hunting owl called out its name. 'Koo-koo-vaya!' it hooted onomatopoeically, 'koo-koo-vaya!' And when it stopped the night seemed even quieter than before.

On the wall in front of me, a spider scuttled into view from behind a paint tin planted with red geraniums. It stopped abruptly, showing black against the whitewash. And as I watched it, the brilliant green head of a lizard appeared above the truss of flowers.

For ten seconds neither stirred. Then slowly, very, very slowly and on silent claws, the lizard crept forward. Closer and closer to its prey it crawled, leg by leg, each limb advanced and placed with exaggerated care. And still the spider did not move.

Five inches from its quarry the lizard stopped, its left leg leading from the right. Then, almost imperceptibly, it cocked its body into an S and for a moment time stood still. There was the faintest of tremors in the lizard's back and then, with the speed of a camera shutter, it struck.

'Koo-koo-vaya!' called the owl once more; and the lizard darted away.

Somehow it seemed a fitting ending to a day full of incident and dramas, imaginary and real. And, I mused as I

shut the gates, in the world of nature the hunting never
stops.

CHAPTER IX

Bangs, Birds and other Beasts

As every reader of *Country Life* and similar glossy magazines which grace doctors' and dentists' waiting rooms will know, August the twelfth is called 'glorious'. It is the day when the voice of the twelve-bore is heard in the land and when that of the grouse is stilled. Nineteen days later the air becomes thick with falling partridge feathers as bucolic gentry especially, and often ridiculously, attired for the occasion, loose off their Purdeys at hitherto protected birds; and then have their photographs taken in company with the dead. But it is in mid-September that the Greek partridge meets its Maker. However, unlike the British the good people of Gennadi do not pose before the camera when the killing stops and, more importantly, they do not particularize upon the appointed day. Excluding domestic animals, they shoot at anything wearing fur or feathers and sometimes, although unintentionally, at one another.

Nor is the twelve-bore their exclusive weapon. Many fine examples of the gunsmith's art are pressed into service. Some are more interesting than others and not necessarily products of this century; but all spell danger to the hunted and, in some cases, to the hunter. And it was the sounds from this assorted arsenal which awoke me early in the morning, accompanied me as I walked once more along the coastal road, and punctured the air until noon.

The gunshots reached me from all directions. They reverberated around the hills, rang out in the fields and banged to my front and cracked to the rear of me. As the Yannis et al had predicted, Gennadi was going 'bam! bam!'

Although quite early in the day the verges already were littered with spent cartridge cases, the sun reflecting off their brass caps, and the road was busy with traffic. Family saloons with gun-barrels sticking out of their side windows and pointing skyward; trucks towing small enclosed trailers with crouching dogs inside them looking like caged mice; mopeds and cycles, their riders festooned with cartridge belts and with shotguns slung across their backs, all sped by me either coming from or going to the hunting fields.

Two gun-carrying pedestrians loped towards me, dead pigeons and partridges swinging from their waists like sporrans. 'Bravo!' I said as we drew abreast and they grinned and thanked me as I carried on. 'Michi rotora!' they shouted over their shoulders – 'it could be worse!' I passed a dead cat on the side of the road, speculated as to whether Panayotis had been abroad, and then stopped at the K.K.E.-bedaubed chapel. Under the tree and sprawled on the circular seat around it was a party of four. Accoutred from head to foot in brown and olive camouflage and wearing green linen hats, their general appearance was that of a commando unit on a sabbatical. And standing near them, and holding a hare by its back legs, was the papas; and his wife. She waved when she saw me and I went over to join them, wondering as I did so, if he had a rook rifle concealed in his robes.

'Kalimerasas,' said the papas, and held up the hare. 'You see,' he smiled, 'the God has been very good.' 'Amin,' responded Mrs Papas automatically, taking the blood-stained corpse from her husband with one hand and crossing herself with the other, 'it will make a fine stew.' 'Ne,' agreed the papas sucking his teeth, 'very tasty.' He beamed benignly upon the most villainous of the quartet. 'A present,' he advised me, 'from him. Unfortunately we do not often see one another in church. However . . .' He left the remainder of the sentence unspoken and nodded appreciatively toward his donor. 'Tipota,' said the lapsed parishioner now doubtlessly assured of his salvation albeit on a temporary basis, 'don't mention it.'

He took a swig from an ouzo bottle, passed it along the line and yawned prodigiously. 'Po! Po! Po!' he said, 'I am very tired. We were up at dawn you understand, but the day has been good.' 'Ne,' said the papas looking at the pile of carcasses at their feet, 'very good.' He turned to me. 'They are excellent shots,' he extolled, 'especially Lefteris. Is that not so?' he asked rhetorically of his lost sheep. 'Ne,' agreed Lefteris immodestly, and rose to his feet. 'You want me to show my skill to the Englishman,' he inquired, anxious to curry more favour in the eyes of the church, 'you wish that he sees?' 'Oche!' said the papas raising his eyebrows and hands simultaneously, 'I do not –'

'Very well!' said Lefteris ignoring the gestures; and cocked his already loaded gun. He signalled towards the now empty bottle in the hands of his nearest companion. 'Throw it up!' he commanded. 'Endaxi!' roared his friend extracting the last drop from it; and hurled it high in the air and over the road. Lefteris hit it with the first barrel.

'Bravo!' exclaimed the papas as the fragments rained down on an elderly passing cyclist, and joined in the round of applause. With the success of the divertissement, he seemed pleased that his original protestation had been overruled. 'And now,' he said, mopping his forehead with the hem of his robe and leaving a dark mark upon his person, 'I think we must go.' 'Ne,' said the company rising together and scratching themselves, 'we must all go – andio!' And slinging their guns and gathering their spoils, they trudged off in the direction of Gennadi.

'And where,' asked the papas's wife as she stuffed the bleeding hare into a polythene bag and a fusillade of shots came from the hills, 'will you walk today?' I said I would go to the beach. For a swim, 'Ne,' said the papas, nodding approvingly, 'that is a good decision. For if you should go into the hills today,' he continued, 'you might very well get shot.' 'Yes,' I said, as more bangs came from up-country, 'you may very well be right.' 'Oh, he is,' said Mrs Papas spitting on her handkerchief and applying it vigorously to her husband's forehead, 'he is.'

The papas was a shrewd old man and obviously knew his territory and the behavioural patterns of his flock upon this day and I did not question his counsel. However, as was to be made manifest to me, patently he had never been moved to take himself to the beaches on this occasion and there lie naked in the sun. Had he done so he would have known that it was not only the hills which were hazardous.

As on the previous day I swam, stretched myself out on the shore by the dried-up river bed and behind closed eyes built castles in the air. Fifteen minutes later their foundations crumbled. A violent bang from somewhere close to the rear of me jerked open my eyes and a shower of buckshot peppered the shingle a few yards from my feet. It was preceded by a terrified rabbit and followed by two dogs. Blind with fear it fled towards the sea, jack-knifed at the water's edge and then ran diagonally back into the gorse with the dogs after it. Within seconds, and baulked of their quarry, they reappeared and rushed towards me barking furiously.

From the ease with which the traumatized rabbit had eluded them I adjudged them to be neither quick-witted nor particularly keen-sighted; but one thing was certain – both knew that they were expected to chase something. I thought of the late and ill-fortuned Actaeon and hastily pulled on my underpants. It was, I reflected, one thing to be bitten fully clad but quite another matter to be savaged in the nude.

Yards from me the leader pulled up with a yelp as a stone hit it behind the ear. 'Piso!' bellowed a voice to my right and both dogs made towards it, fawning and wagging their tails. 'Urrgh!' shouted their owner, brandishing his fire-arm at them, 'you are rubbish! You understand? rubbish!'

He was a powerfully built, porcine looking gentleman with a very small close-cropped head, strabismus in one eye and wearing a check shirt across which was slung a bandolier with but two cartridges in it. I would not have had him in my drawing room.

'Yasu!' he growled at me, 'I am sorry about the dogs but they would not have eaten you.' 'Thenbarazi,' I said, totally unconvinced and adjusting my Y-fronts the while, 'but have you had a good day?' 'Oche!' he said spitting in one direction and looking in the other, 'I have hit nothing! Tipota!' he reiterated raising his voice and gesticulating wildly and causing the dogs to cower, 'and do you know why?' He thumped his fist frustratedly against his chest. 'It is because of my glasses! My glasses you understand! They fell off my nose and broke when I trod on them! Into small pieces! That is why I have hit nothing!' The two dogs looked at each other and sniggered. 'And that,' said their master morosely, 'is why now I am going home.' He shouldered his fowling-piece disgruntledly. 'Maybe I try again tomorrow,' he said. And calling to his curs he nodded curtly to me and the three of them slouched away with their tails between their legs. I hoped for everyone's sake that the spirit would not move him on the morrow.

The incident had unsettled me. Conscious of my narrow deliverance and thinking that all cross-eyed men with or without optical aids should be prevented by legislation from using fire-arms, I finished dressing and began to walk back to Gennadi. Moreover, not only did I keep to the beach – I walked in the sea.

'Yasu Jono!' called Pavlos in a mixture of Greek and Australian as I trudged up the sand towards Klimi's, 'how you doing mate – kala?' I told him of my experience. He thought it was very droll and laughed immoderately. 'My oath,' he said, 'You'd have looked funny with your arse full of holes.' He lit a cigarette and blew the match out in one motion. 'Still, that's nothing,' he said, 'some joker shot a bloody goat this morning . . . .'

The taverna was well patronized that lunchtime. The papas's friends had long since arrived and were dozing at a table under a tree, Christos and Baba Yanni were present; and so was Bugs Bunny. But it was Baba Yanni who excited my attention. Unlike his son-in-law Christos, he had eschewed the much favoured camouflage clothing and was dressed in an off-white shirt. He had also retained his flat hat under which he was smiling contentedly; and with good reason. Around his waist and below his cartridge belt hung the corpses of several small birds.

'Bravo,' I said as I greeted them, 'you have done well!' 'Ne,' grinned Baba Yanni standing up, 'in truth we have!' 'How many?' I asked, pointing to his scalp-belt. 'Twenty-three,' he said delightedly, and turned on his axis like an elderly hula-hula dancer making the little birds fan out in a fringe. 'Would you like some, Yanni – for your meal tonight?' He did not wait for the answer but unhooked four of them from his belt and passed them to me. 'They are delicious,' he said. 'You eat all of their parts you understand? Except the beak. And the head is the best of all.' 'Ne,' agreed Christos taking off his dark glasses and wiping them, 'very crunchy.' 'Poli!' accorded Bugs Bunny; and chewed his tongue. 'Yum-yum!' he said, 'poli yum-yum!'

I looked at the small, plump, and still warm bodies cupped between my hands. They had grey crowns and rumps and their upper parts were chocolate brown and streaked with black. 'Are they not sparrows?' I asked. 'Ne,' confirmed Christos, 'sparithe!' 'Ne,' said Bugs Bunny assuming the role of general effects man, 'cheep! cheep! Take them to Katrina in the kitchen. She will pluck and cook them for you for this evening.' I thanked Baba Yanni for his kindness and carried the little birds inside.

'Po! po! po!' said fat Katrina when she saw them, and shook her head. 'So many feathers,' she sighed, 'and for such little flesh.'

That evening as I sat between the two Yannis and facing Christos, I stared at the unhappy foursome upon my plate. Katrina's preparation of them had been very thorough but Klimi's presentation lacked finesse. They were served to me lying on their backs with their feet sticking up and the heads, complete with bulging eyeballs, turned sideways. Undressed they looked even more pathetic than when feathered and for the first time in my life I considered vegetarianism.

'Kali orexi!' said Baba Yanni as I continued to look at them. He beamed encouragingly at me like an unshaven Norland Nanny. And conscious that his and other eyes were upon me I licked my lips, disabused myself of the vision of Cronos devouring his children and ate the first of the innocents.

It was, as Baba Yanni had prognosticated, delicious. Especially the head. I attacked the second without squeamishness.

'Were they not a good meze?' Baba Yanni inquired as I put the last beak on the side of the plate, 'did you not enjoy them?' 'Greatly,' I said, and thanked him again for his generosity.

Christos cleared his throat. 'Do you not have sparrows in London?' he asked, politely. 'Yes,' I said, 'we do. In thousands, perhaps millions.' 'But you do not shoot or net them?' pursued Christos perplexedly. 'Nor eat them?' asked Baba Yanni, equally puzzled. I shook my head. 'No,' I said, 'we neither shoot nor eat sparrows in London.' There was a short silence while this eccentricity of the English was digested and analysed. It was broken by Bugs Bunny. 'Perhaps,' he suggested, 'it is because the Thatcher does not approve of such things.' 'Perhaps,' I said, rising from the table, 'we should have another bottle of retsina.' My Greek was tolerable but already I had been found wanting when it came to discussing politics in general and those of the Thatcher in particular.

I took my dirty plate to the kitchen, asked Katrina for something more substantial to join the sparrows, and helped myself to a bottle from Klimi's refrigerator under his counter. Inside the taverna three German visitors were watching a television interview featuring Mrs Thatcher speaking in English to the Greek Prime Minister. 'Ah,' said one of them as I moved closer to the set, 'your Maggi Thatcher, ya? She is, how you say, the iron nut – isn't it?' 'Yes,' I said, 'but I understand she's very fond of sparrows.' And made my way outside.

As I crossed to the table two shooting-brakes drew up in quick succession and shed their passengers. From the first came a noisy party of two men, two women with an accordion, and from the second, a small wiry man and two dogs. Freed from their confinement they rushed down to the sea kicking up the sand in spurts and barking joyously as they ran. The driver slammed the car door shut and stood for a moment in profile to me looking towards the animals in the fading light. Hook-nosed and finely chiselled and topped by a head of thick grey wavy hair, his features were magnificent. Arrogant and aquiline, it was a face not easily forgotten and as I admired it, suddenly I remembered where I had seen it in the past. It had been three years before, in Karpathos, at the Post Office party in Othos – he it was who had helped to tie the stricken Apostoli's moustachios together. And I remembered his name.

'Evangelos!' I called. He jerked his head towards me and stared hard. Then, as he recognized me he raised his hands. 'Oche!' he shouted in disbelief, 'it is not possible! Yanni!' And moving quickly towards each other we met in the centre of the taverna and embraced.

'Yanni mu!' he said as we drew apart, 'what brings you here?' I told him and reversed the question. For a year, he said, he had been stationed in Rhodes and today he had been hunting with a friend, in the hills. He pointed to a huge black-bearded man wearing a leather jacket and a cap with ear-flaps who was standing by the car and whistling to the dogs. 'Tito!' he called – 'ella!' 'I come,' rumbled the giant as the dogs returned obediently and jumped into the car; and slamming the door on them he walked slowly towards us.

He reached us at the same time as the trio of departing Germans. 'Forgive me,' said their leader who was unmistakably Teutonic, 'but we are not so well understanding the business of Thatcher and the sparrows.' I explained the origination as succinctly as I could. 'I thought it was quite funny,' I said. He looked at me blankly and translated the account to his companions. 'Thank you,' he said when he had finished, 'we do not think it so funny. Gute Nacht.'

Tito watched them stalk away and then took my extended hand as Evangelos acquainted us. 'Ya,' he said; but there was little warmth in his voice; nor in his handshake. By contrast Evangelos bubbled like a boiling kettle. From the moment I introduced them to the Yannis and Christos and they joined us at the table, he held sway and laughed infectiously as he enlightened the company as to how we had met on that memorable night in Othos. And as the embellished story of Apostoli and his moustachios unfolded so the laughter swelled. Glasses were replenished, food arrived and the talk became general and louder. They spoke about matters of which I knew nothing, but they all included me in the conversation. All save Tito.

Sitting opposite to me and next to Christos he barely acknowledged my presence and never once did he address me directly. I began to feel uncomfortable and wondered if it had been by accident that he had not clinked glasses with me when, in turn with the others, I had contributed a bottle. I became increasingly ill at ease and I started to hum. It was a reflex action. Since childhood I have always hummed when feeling unsure or under stress. But it was fate which chose the tune.

'When is the weather going to clear so I will be able to take my rifle, the beautiful Patrona? I will go down the mountain, to the village of Omalo, and there I will make mothers without sons, women without husbands . . . .'

That is the gist of the song I hummed. It is from Crete – a wild, passionate, sad and revolutionary song which the Cretans have sung since before the days when they rose against the Turks.

I got no further than the first two bars. There was a crash as Tito knocked his glass to the floor and seized me by the wrist. 'Oriste!' cried Christos as the wine spilt over him; and the conversation faltered, and died.

Tito's grip was like a vice. 'That song,' he said, leaning towards me and barely audible, 'how do you know it?' Intense dark eyes burned into mine. 'I learned it from friends,' I said, 'Cretan friends. I made many when I visited the graves at Souda Bay.' He drew in his breath and his grip tightened. 'Then you are not, German?' 'Oche,' I said, 'I'm English.' 'Oh God,' he said; and closed his eyes, his brow furrowed in self-reproach. 'My friend I am so sorry, so very sorry. You see, I thought –' And standing up he grasped me in a bear hug across the table, embraced me and then drew back.

'You remember the fighting in Crete,' he asked, his hands still on my shoulders, 'the battles?' 'Yes,' I said. 'And I remember the courage of the Cretans.' 'Ne,' he said, 'ne. I was twelve then, a partisan, you understand. So was my brother. They cut off one of his ears and then shot him – in front of my mother. Ma to theo – I tell the truth! But that song, I sang it many times . . .' And standing to attention, and in a voice darker than a thousand midnights he started to sing. He sang with a passion that came from the heart and the tears rolled down his cheeks. And one by one the taverna rose until not one was seated. Christos, Yanni, Evangelos, Lukas, the accordion party in the corner – all sang the song of Crete.

It was a moment which will never be erased from my memory. And when it was done and the applause had died, fresh bottles appeared and we sang again but this time in a lighter vein – of Marias and Yannis and love and peace, and accompanied by the accordion. And Tito danced with a glass on his head and hissed through his teeth as the Cretans will, and Evangelos whistled and shouted and clapped, and the Yannis danced with each other.

Eventually the party broke up. Christos and the Yannis went their separate ways, I swore undying friendship with Tito and waved to him and Evangelos as they drove away to Rhodes, and then went in to see Klimi. 'What fun that was,' I said, and produced my wallet. Klimi grunted. 'Ne,' he agreed grudgingly as he totted up my bill, 'your friends were very happy. They had the kephi,' he said, using the word for which there is no equivalent in English, 'poli!' He grunted again over the figures. 'They were very lucky you understand; such things cannot be planned. They can only happen when the kephi comes – that is when men dance. Symphonis Yanni?' 'Ne,' I said as he handed me my change, 'I agree. But you did not have the kephi.'

Klimi stared at me across the counter. 'Me?' he said, stabbing his chest with his finger, 'the kephi?' How can I have the kephi? He gesticulated angrily and repeated the

Tito danced with a glass on his head.

question. 'I have no time to drink because there is too much work, Maria has gone to our daughter in Rhodes and left me alone until Saturday and also,' he continued, clasping his face, 'I have a bad tooth. A very bad tooth, Yanni,' he emphasized – 'see for yourself.' And opening his mouth wide and holding his breath he pointed to a lower molar in the rear and invited me to make a closer inspection. I peered into the cavern and beyond two gold-capped incisors, and then drew back hurriedly as he exhaled. 'Oh dear,' I said, 'I see what you mean.'

'And that is not all,' said Klimi resuming his catalogue of woes and hoisting his leg on to a chair, 'I still ache where I was bitten.' He pulled up his trouser leg to expose his calf. 'You see?' he said, 'it is still very pink.' He straightened up. 'Maria said that I should have had an immediate injection in the bottom and because I did not I may go mad by Sunday.' Rapidly he crossed himself. 'Please the God I do not go mad by Sunday,' he invoked, 'it is Maria Micri's christening day.' I looked at him inquiringly. 'Our grand-daughter,' he explained, 'Little Maria.' And produced a photograph.

'Ah,' I said, glad of better news and admiring it, 'bravo! And may the child live for you,' I added, not because I doubted Maria Micri's ability to survive until the Sabbath but because it is the traditional wish at such time, 'na sas zisi!' 'Epharisto!' said Klimi brightening up, 'and you will come to the church on Sunday? To rejoice with us? At five o'clock?' 'I will,' I said, 'epharisto poli.' And assuring him that I thought it most unlikely that he would be potty by Sunday, I made my way home pondering as I did so that even if his sanity did leave him, his halitosis would be by far the greater social drawback at the function.

I walked into a very dark night with neither stars nor

moon to light my way and the air was oppressive and still. Somewhere beyond the hills sheet lightning played above the clouds and thunder rumbled in the distance. I thought how foolish I had been not to have brought a torch and wished that my night vision was as good as the cat's which scuttled across my path, its eyes flashing green as it stopped in its tracks to face me.

It was at the top of the hill past the cafeneon that I saw my first light. It was soft and glimmered from a doorway on the right. Then, as I walked towards it, other lights appeared from the opposite side of the road. They moved and flickered through the darkness and then went out, and as I drew nearer to them I heard the murmur of muted voices and began to see the shadowy shapes of women, each carrying a candle. They crossed quietly to the open doorway, and went in. By its entrance stood three lounge-suited sentinels with stiff white collars and wearing ties. I stopped, halted by the incongruity of their appearance.

The three heads turned slowly toward me. 'Kalinichta,' I said to the pinstriped gentleman nearest to me, and made to move on. He bowed gravely in return and gestured solemnly towards the door. 'Won't you please come in, sir,' he said in a low voice and in English, 'there are still one or two seats.' I hesitated. 'Please,' he said, 'you will be most welcome;' and ushered me in.

It was an interesting if Kafkaesque spectacle which greeted me. The four walls of the room, which was candle-lit, were lined by two rows of hard-backed chairs occupied by sombrely clad men and women, and three small children. Two were sucking their thumbs and the third, a lollipop. The centre of the room was occupied by a middle-aged gentleman also attired in an outmoded single-breasted pinstripe and wearing shiny black boots. I had often seen his like standing and smiling waxily at me through the windows of Moss Bros and, in days long gone, the Fifty Shilling Tailors. There was however one important difference between them. This gentleman was unsmiling and lying down. He was very dead. At his head sat his widow, red-eyed and weeping quietly into a handkerchief and flanked by four other ladies similarly employed.

'Will you come this way please, sir,' said my guide, and showed me to a vacant second row seat to the right of the door. I sat down. 'Coffee, sir?' he inquired; and eased his collar with his forefinger. I nodded affirmatively and automatically. 'Black?' he asked hollowly. 'Of course,' I said; and mopped my forehead. The atmosphere was stifling.

My host returned. 'Did you know him in life, sir?' he asked, passing me a cup and nodding towards the guest of honour. I shook my head. 'Stephano,' he said by way of introduction. 'He died last week. In Melbourne. On holiday.' He cleared his throat. 'Three thousand five hundred Australian dollars it cost to bring him home embalmed,' he intoned, 'and our air fares,' he added. 'But he would not have wished to stay in Australia. Not permanently.' His voice dropped half an octave. 'Stephano will be buried tomorrow', he said. He cleared his throat again. 'Would you like a biscuit?' he asked.

The second mention of Stephano's name brought a fresh outbreak of sobbing from his widow and provoked a chain reaction among the assembled. The child with the lollipop choked on the bon-bon and was led out by its parents and two more mourners took their places, disturbing the air as they did so. The candle flames flickered and the shadows jumped on the whitewashed walls, and I sat sipping but not tasting my coffee and let the soft sounds of grief wash over me.

'Parakalo,' said the lady next to me when I handed her my cup and eased past her. I stood for a moment by the side of the body with my head bowed. I said a short prayer, crossed myself in Greek fashion and was conscious of the murmur of understanding as I did so. I turned to the widow. 'May God bless and be with you,' I said. 'Episis,' she said through her handkerchief; 'and thank you for coming in.'

I left in a daze and a confusion of thought, wondering as I walked if the affair had been a dream and not reality. Was it possible, I asked myself, that I, a total stranger, had been ushered as if into a cinema to view the corpse of a man I had never met, and had prayed for the soul of someone I had never known? And had a widow really thanked me for 'coming in' to share her vigil? But the event had happened and I was glad that I had been privy to the scene for it had underlined what I already knew – the strength of family unity in Greece. The man who loved his country and his village had been brought home, and relatives and friends abroad had made the journey with him. And there, in a humble roughcast room they had cosseted his widow and given her strength in her hour of need. Nor, I reflected, would she ever be alone. The dead would be buried, but she would be cherished; and that moment in particular she would never forget; the hours when she was made aware that others cared about her grief. The overt Greek style of mourning may be bizarre to English eyes but in many ways it is more efficacious than repressed sadness behind closed doors on which no callers knock.

I was talking to Pavlos when the bell tolled for Stephano the following day. 'Poor old bastard,' he said, looking towards the sound, 'it cost them a packet to bring him back. My word it did.' He extracted a battered cigarette from his shirt pocket and straightened it. 'Still, that's the way it goes, Jono. My Ma and Pa like Aussie fair enough but they wouldn't want to be planted out there. My oath they wouldn't.' He flicked his lighter and inhaled. 'I hear you dropped in on him last night?' 'Yes,' I said, 'but it was more by accident than design. 'Yeah?' said Pavlos taking a shred of tobacco off his tongue, 'well, it was much appreciated, mate. Especially by the old lady.' He stopped as a thought struck him.

'Oh my word,' he said; and started to giggle – 'imagine doing that in Pomsville. . . .'

CHAPTER X

Fears, Fonts and Fond Farewells

FORTUNATELY FOR MY nervous system, that day and the following ones were free from trauma. Stephano was buried, Yiorgo recovered from his imaginary bereavement as a cat does from a false pregnancy, and the bangs grew fewer as the initial enthusiasm waned. No one shot at or near me, neither was I invited to view corpses nor television, and the only drama to occur on the Friday was provided by Lukas and Poppi's small son Yiorgo. Shortly before six o'clock he swallowed a safety pin and was upended and belaboured and shaken on the doorstep by an hysterical Poppi. Within thirty seconds he had attracted an audience of seven women, four children, Panayotis and two dogs all of whom screamed, shouted or barked advice, until at a minute past the hour, he regurgitated the object to a relieved chorus of Aahs, Bravos and Po! po! po!s. Excluding the dogs and Panayotis all the assembled crossed themselves, Panayotis produced a bottle of ouzo, stuck it first under the nose of Yiorgo, then beneath Poppi's, and lastly between his own lips. He replaced the cork with unsteady fingers. 'Such things,' he advised me as the company dispersed, 'agitate me and upset my stomach.' The incident must have preyed upon him for he was still in need of solace when I saw him briefly twenty-four hours later towards the end of another uneventful but happy day.

It was a day of which I had spent the greater part walking in the hills around Gennadi to which I returned tired but content an hour before the sun went down. And I remember it especially for its dying hours. For the smell of incense drifting from the church and from the private censers in the houses; for the sounds of an old lady thinly singing to herself before an icon as I passed her open door and saw the glimmer of a single candle; for the love and devotion which showed in the face of an elderly man as he wheeled his mute and crippled brother with fine moustachios and lustrous eyes into the cafeneon where Panayotis toped; but above all for a little child named Yanni.

Yanni was a fair-haired rickety little boy of about two and a half with big brown eyes with long sweeping lashes and a face badly swollen by mosquito bites. Each evening he would sit with his comfortable mother Komisa outside the gate of their tiny house and from the first day of my arrival I had said hallo to them as I passed by on my way to or from the beach. He had been thrilled that we bore the same name and by the second day, and encouraged by his mother, he had overcome his shyness and we became friends. He had shown me his most treasured possession, a faded blue and green feather from a roller and had stroked my face with it and chortled when I reacted to the tickling.

'Yasu Yannaki mu!' I said, 'ti kanete? Kala?' 'Poli kala,' said Komisa answering on his behalf, 'and see what he has to show you! Ella Yannaki,' she said encouragingly as I squatted down beside them, 'will you show Yanni your pictures?' The child looked at me from where he sat on his mother's lap and for a moment sucked his thumb in deliberation. Then nodding vigorously he pushed his treasures towards me. 'Epharisto poli,' I said, and picked them up. They were garish, badly reproduced picture postcards of saints and other religious memorabilia.

'Are they not beautiful?' asked Komisa as I thumbed through them. 'Very beautiful,' I assured her insincerely but diplomatically as I gazed for a decent interval at each photographic blasphemy before slipping it to the bottom of the pack, 'most attractive. And holy,' I added unctuously. The last and worst of the reproductions faced me. It was the Madonna and Child.

'Da!' said Yannaki leaning forward and rubbing a wet and grimy finger over the Blessed Virgin's face – 'orea!' Komisa beamed. 'His favourite,' she said; and kissed him on the head. 'And do you know who she is?' I asked him. 'Ne,' said Yannaki opening wide his big brown eyes and nodding – 'Theotokou.' Komisa beamed again. 'Ne,' she said, 'he knows, he knows!' And gave him a little hug. 'And that?' I asked, pointing to the Infant Christ in the Virgin's arms and expecting him to say 'yes, the baby Jesus,' 'do you know who the child is?' 'Ne,' he said, 'I know.' And sitting up in his mother's lap, slowly he gimleted first one palm with a podgy finger, and then the other. Then spreading his chubby arms wide in the attitude of crucifixion, he lolled his head limply back on to one side, closed his eyes and opened his mouth. It was a dreadfully telling piece of mime and one which staggered me, coming as it did from one so young. At that age, I reflected as I continued on my way to an early supper, my image of the Christchild had been coloured by cosy Tarrant illustrations pinned to a nursery wall.

Down at Klimi's I watched the sun sink below the hills, bronzing the landscape and the sands and listened to the chatter of roosting birds in the almirithra tree under which I sat. At that hour the taverna was all but deserted and for the first time since my arrival I ate alone and left early. The day's walking had left me very weary and I longed for bed.

'Do not forget tomorrow,' said Klimi as I departed, 'Maria Micri's christening!' His face was still swollen like that of a hamster with a full cheek pouch but he seemed happier than of late and was obviously relieved that despite Maria's Cassandra-like prognosis he had, to date, shown no signs of hydrophobia. Also, Maria had returned from Rhodes. 'Ne,' said she, her hair already in curlers in ample preparation for Gennadi's social event of the year, 'do not forget! Five o'clock tomorrow afternoon. At the church. And then here!' 'Endaxi,' I said, smothering a yawn, 'I'll be there – at five o'clock. Kalinichta!' 'Sweet dreams,' said Maria taking a quick roll-call of her curlers, and turned to her husband. 'Your face is dreadful,' she said, 'also your breath is bad. It is all to do with the dog,' she persisted, 'you should have had an injection. Had you had an injection in your bottom then your breath wouldn't smell. Symphonis Yanni?' she inquired. I left hurriedly. Maria's logic was equalled only by her obsession with injections.

I slept well and long that night, awakening in time to hear the chattering of old men and women and children as they passed the house on their return from the church around the corner. All exchanged greetings with me as I stood at the gate watching them go by in twos and threes, some munching on the pieces of holy bread which the papas had given them at the end of the service. One or two of them offered me a piece and others gave me sprigs of basil or cut flowers but all found time to say good morning.

'And why,' said Anthi and Thespe as they stopped, 'were you not at church this morning? Two days ago when you cracked the almonds with us you said you would be!' 'Ah,' I said, hanging my head in mock shame, 'I overslept. But I shall be there this afternoon.' 'Then-barazi,' said Thespe, moving on, 'I said a prayer for you!' 'And so did I,' said Anthi not to be outdone, and gave me a gauze packet before catching up with her friend. It contained a mixture of meal, cinnamon, almonds, pomegranate seeds, silver balls and sugar. I had no idea of its religious significance but it was delicious with yoghourt.

I was indolent that day. Predictably I walked to my secluded part of the beach, swam for an hour, whiled away the time by watching two men and a boy fishing with hand lines from a dinghy close to the shore, picked some wild grapes from a ground-hugging sprawling vine in a stubble field and returned to the house to snooze until, late in the afternoon, I hosed myself down from the stand pipe in the courtyard and made myself presentable for the event to come.

Foolishly I arrived punctually at the church. Foolish because I had known Greece long enough to realize that to the Greeks time is only an idea in the mind of God. When a Greek says that he will meet you at such an hour the statement should not be interpreted literally. What the speaker really means, and with no thought of deceit, is that at the appointed hour and with the proviso that he is awake, he will think about meeting you and then begin preparations to keep the appointment. It is a national trait manifest in all strata of Greek society and best exampled by employees of bus companies, air and ferry services, but in

'*I said a prayer for you!*'
'*And so did I.*'

no way undemonstrated at private and public functions. Consequently I was not surprised to find that apart from an elderly tom-cat engaged in desecrating the door of the deserted church, I was the only person outside the building at five o'clock.

I knew the cat. It was a tortoiseshell with half a tail, one ear and a built-in expression of malevolence and I had long concluded that it was socially unacceptable in the village. However I passed the time of day with it and sat on the wall to wait for something to happen. It did.

At a quarter past five the wrought iron gates of the churchyard opened and in walked a wild-eyed young man dressed in a sports coat and an open-necked shirt. He stopped when he saw me and then came forward. 'I know you,' he shouted in fractured English as he advanced, 'but you do not know me!' He banged his chest. 'I am the papas's son. You understand? The papas's son. Oh yes. I ring the bell! Bim-ba-bom!' he illustrated pulling an imaginary rope above his head with both hands and pointing to the belfry, 'also I sing, read from the books, give out bread, take money and carry the Cross. I am,' he said, concluding the recitation of his versatility, 'very important.'

He glared at me as if daring me to disagree with him. 'And you know other things about me,' he asked, still shouting, 'I tell you! I worked in Athens. With airways. See I show you!' He fished into an inner pocket and produced an identification photograph in a cellophane jacket. 'That me,' he said, jabbing at it. 'Two year I work airways. Then one day I take all papers and tickets from many people, tear them to little pieces and throw them in air. Ha! ha! I say – now where hell you go? Ha! ha! I tell them now you walk, yes? Rome, Istanbul, Paris, Stuttgart

– all places you bloody walk, ha! ha! Then I go hospital. They say "Ah! breakdown of nerves – send him home, quick!" And so,' concluded this verger/acolyte/sexton extraordinaire, replacing the souvenir of his past employment, 'I come!' He paused. 'My father say me you very good man,' he said; and extended his hand. 'I am pleased for you to meet me; thank-you-very-much-bye-bye!' And turning on his heels he broke into a run and disappeared inside the bell-tower. Seconds later he reappeared on the ramparts like a latter-day Quasimodo. 'Now I begin,' he shouted down to me, and divesting himself of his jacket he seized the bell toggle and crashed the clapper against the side. The cat watched him dispassionately, yawned, sniffed at the church door, and christened it for the second time.

As the peals rang out with all the urgency of an old fashioned fire engine on its way to a conflagration, the papas arrived accompanied by his wife carrying two plastic detergent buckets. They wished me good afternoon, the cat to perdition and entered the church. Five minutes later Demos the Vet appeared deep in conversation with his fiancée whose figure suggested that they had anticipated their marriage by several months, so did Baba Yanni, and Christos with his wife; and so did a motley collection of children mostly dressed like angels but all behaving like devils incarnate. Hopping, skipping, screaming and fighting they became increasingly diabolical as the minutes passed. An eight year old girl looking as if she had been plucked from the top of a Christmas tree and carrying a monstrous candle decorated with pink and white frills, was wantonly attacked by Poppi's Yiorgo, retaliated by striking him about the head with the giant artefact, was pulled from her fallen victim before she could administer the coup de grâce, and promptly burst into tears of frustration. Poppi said 'there there', straightened the candle and rearranged the frills, smacked Yiorgo for good measure to cheers from the surrounding demons; and at five-thirty the christening party arrived.

Through the gates came Maria Micri in the arms of her mother, then her father and her godfather, a red-faced Klimi sucking cachous with his Maria coiffured tightly, and lastly but by no means least, a coachload of relatives from Rhodes. Aunts and uncles, nieces, nephews, cousins more than once removed, old and young all smelling sweetly, freshly washed and newly laundered, all mustered chattering in the square. Then, as the bell clanged to an undisciplined stop and Quasimodo reappeared jacketed once more and ready to perform another of his many duties, the last cigarettes were ground underfoot and we surged into the church in a solid perspiring phalanx.

I intend no irreverence, but even to Anglican eyes accustomed to, and acquainted with, many of the rituals of the Greek Orthodox Church, the proceedings that followed were, to say the least, unusual. As Shakespeare advised us, it is neither advantageous nor productive to make comparisons, but nevertheless I could not recall having attended a baptism in Britain where the congregation talked and pursued their own devices with scant regard to what the priest or choir were doing or singing, and where children romped around a half-assembled font paying off old scores. One child stood out in particular. Dressed in a T-shirt which advised the reader that she was a Rotten Punk and working in tandem with another she-devil whose vest proclaimed that she approved of Moose Head Beer, she possessed the best right hook in the Dodecanese and within two minutes between them they had floored two whey-faced acolytes and forced a third to seek running repairs.

Nor until that day had I ever seen a font actually erected on site.

Four buxom ladies dressed in black, two of whom clearly had differing ideas from their sisters as to the modus operandi, addressed themselves vigorously but inexpertly to the task and presented me with an entirely new understanding of the old saw about what happens when Greek meets Greek. However, eventually their labours triumphed and the buzz of appreciative and congratulatory comment reached a new peak. The heavy-weight quartet modestly acknowledged the applause and leaned upon the contraption to verify its stability.

'Endaxi?' inquired the papas from where he was standing behind it with the godfather. 'Endaxi,' confirmed his wife, smacking her hands together. And adjusting her small round dark glasses, she seized the first of the two plastic buckets which stood by the font. Wizened little body she may have been but under her white scarf there was the strength of ten men. Up went the container labelled DAZ, in went its contents of boiling water, up went its companion containing cold and propounding the virtues of TIDE; and up went the sleeves of Mrs Papas.

'Ladle!' she called imperiously as would a surgeon in an operating theatre; and agitating the waters she vanished momentarily in a cloud of steam. 'More cold,' she commanded reappearing through the mist and wiping her fogged spectacles as the addition was made, and then, in the best tradition of all good nannies stuck her elbow in the font. 'Endaxi,' she pronounced. 'Endaxi,' echoed the papas enriching the mixture with a tumbler of oil; and the service commenced. The papas began the intoning of the ritual prayers, the choir of two started the chant which was to last throughout the proceedings, and those nearest to the scene of action continued to give a ball by ball commentary to the less favoured spectators in the rear.

Up to that point, Maria Micri, shortly to become the cynosure but happily innocent of that fact, was at peace with the world. Unmoved and comfortable in her mother's arms she watched a party of chattering women and adolescents unpack a large cardboard carton from which they drew forth her brand new christening clothes, all of which had price tags adhering to them. She did not even join in the cries of appreciation with which the appearance of each garment was greeted. Instead she continued to savour the delights of a posy of paper flowers with which she was being fed by a little girl with the face of a Botticelli angel but whose mien belied her true nature.

For an eighteen month old child Maria Micri had a remarkably large mouth with an exceptional capacity. When her bonne-bouche was discovered only the silver papered stems remained visible; but it was a pity that the espial was made for with it vanished the last vestiges of decorum. With a scream of 'Mana mu! Look what she's eating,' which topped the combined vocal contributions of all present and arrested the display of Maria Macri's lingerie and brought the exhibitors rushing towards her, her mother pulled out the mangled remains and flung the sodden remnants to the floor. Robbed of her bonbonnière Maria Micri opened her vermilion stained mouth wide with surprise, inhaled deeply to give vent to her feelings and immediately had the opening replugged with a dummy.

It was an unwise move. Close to asphyxiation, Maria Micri went blue, her mother turned white, everyone screamed and for the next two minutes the scene took on an aspect associated more with a scrum-down at the Cardiff Arms Park than with a religious ceremony in a place of worship. To shrieks from Poppi, who was acting as prop-forward, of 'this is what happened to Yiorgo,' Maria Micri was inverted, banged on the back, poked in the stomach and at one point disappeared from view. Seconds later, and with the swiftness of a ball being passed along the line, she emerged from the mêlée minus her dress, arrived at the font where a disposable nappy was whipped from under her with a speed which must have left scorch marks, and scarlet and bellowing with incarnate rage, was presented to the papas. Deftly, and sagely removing his hearing aid, he gathered her to him, anointed her forehead, her limbs, her back and her front, replaced the dummy, and plunged her thrice into the cauldron making the sign of the cross with his nose as he did so.

Even before Maria Micri had suffered her first immersion she had not been pleased by the sequence of events. Nor when she surfaced for the last time and her dummy was again removed before she was handed over to her godfather, had her appreciation of the situation changed. Still finding the proceedings less than amusing she demonstrated her feelings uninhibitedly and as only a baby can. Smiling wanly, her godfather, now resplendent in thick white turkish towelling, set about the drying of his goddaughter; and his person. Meanwhile the papas, accepting the offer of a bar of pink soap fashioned in the image of a she-child, manufactured a healthy lather, scrubbed up, and dried his hands on the godfather's garment. For Maria Micri however, the ritual was not yet over.

Barely visible through a cloud of talcum powder but still moist and sticky despite the efforts of her godfather she was handed back to the papas. He, secure in the knowledge that she was unlikely to perpetrate a second enormity within so brief a spell, held her high above his head to receive her new clothes and to assist in the attiring. Unfortunately, well meaning though his efforts were, they fell short of perfection largely through lack of rehearsal.

Easing her head through the armhole of a pristine white embroidered vest marked 180 Drs. and realizing his mistake, he withdrew it and allowed his wife to guide it through the right aperture and Maria Micri's arms through the others. Nor was he happy with the frilly pants. These he drew upon her back to front, recognized his error and pulled them off, and then replaced them correctly, but inside out. Happily he enjoyed greater success with both the petticoat and dress. The white socks however presented him with a further problem mainly because they were still joined together with thread. These were seized by Mrs Papas who separating them by chewing through the connecting cord, coaxed them on to the squirming feet and from then on it was plain sailing. Red shoes were fitted and buttoned over the socks, a cotton bonnet half a size too big was placed on her head and tied under her chin, and her white dress was surmounted by a heavy velvet maroon cape with an outsized hood. Prolonged applause greeted the completion of the enrobing. The velvet hood was pulled into position over the bonnet causing it to tilt drunkenly over Maria Micri's right eye, and perspiring freely, but now silent, she peered beadily through the left one and into the lens of a battery of clicking cameras as she was lifted on to the shoulders of her godfather.

'Bravo!' cried the assembled on an ever rising tide, 'na sas zisi – may the child live!' And as the cheers rang out and the flash bulbs popped and the more pietistic fell to their knees, so Demos the Vet accompanied by three equally muscular stalwarts, rushing from the rear of the church and clasping Maria Micri's godfather under his buttocks, hoisted the two of them above their heads and ran with them towards the altar screen. Maria Micri gave a tipsy smile, stretched out a podgy hand as if to touch the face of God and the congregation cheered anew. 'Amin,' said the papas now repossessed of his hearing aid, and crossed himself. 'Amin,' echoed his wife, adjusting it with the help of her son who had hurried from the lectern, 'amin!'

'Is she not like an angel?' exclaimed Maria above the hubbub, her eyes bright with fervour as she presented me with an apoplectic blue-checked gingham doll filled with sugared almonds and thrust a sponge finger into my mouth, 'and is it all not wonderful?' 'Truly it is,' I said through a mouthful of crumbs; and watched the papas's son sprinting to the belfry to ring down the curtain. And it was.

It had been hot in the church but outside it was equally close and humid. I looked towards Maria Micri still perched on her godfather's shoulder. Hooded and cocooned in her heavy velvet, I wondered how long it would be before she melted; but her resilience seemed greater than his. Visibly he was wilting; but not so his goddaughter. Quick to forget and to forgive the indignities to which she had been subjected during the past hour, she was in rare good humour. Chuckling and cooing, gurgling and dribbling, she was doing her best to remove her godfather's moustache, hair by hair. Excluding the godparent everyone said how sweet she was and continued to enjoy his discomforture until we all formed up to process back to the taverna.

'Endaxi?' enquired the papas from the head of the chattering crocodile. 'Endaxi,' confirmed his perspiring son as he arrived panting from the belfry to take his place by his father's side, and off we moved with the immediate family to the fore.

Sedately we processed through the village, singing as we went. From time to time the papas's voice faltered and he was forced to take a few bars' rest; but not so his son; nor the elderly retired schoolmaster on the other side of him. Bravely they chanted and sang without a break, as did two other men with fine bass voices and healthy lungs. And as we walked the dusty downhill three quarters of a mile to Klimi's and dogs barked as we passed them by and seated villagers outside their houses respectfully stood and crossed themselves, I reflected on what a strange mixture of levity, devotion, and religious observance the ceremony had been; and how privileged I was to have been invited to be part of it. But the festivities were not yet over.

Back at the taverna the tables had been laid and arranged in long lines by Lukas and Pavlos who had not attended the service. As Pavlos put it, he wasn't into christenings and anyway the incense got up his nose, my word it did. 'Kathiste!' cried Klimi as Maria Micri was whisked into the kitchen to be given a much needed quick service in the sink by her grandmother, 'everyone sit down!'

And there we sat – the entire congregation. Old and young, friends and relations, and addressed ourselves to meze, meatballs, mousakas and chicken legs all served together on one large plate and washed down with cans of beer. Maria Micri reappeared in company with her grandmother and a vast christening cake over which she was dangled whilst it was sliced and passed around and ingested; the papas gave a vote of thanks, everyone drummed on their plates with their knives and forks; and a child sitting opposite me was led away to be sick.

'Dear me,' said the papas, noting its change of colour and preparing to take his leave, 'it must have been the cake. It was,' he added, and with difficulty through goo-encrusted dentures, 'very rich.'

Towards the north-west the sun sank lower and as it went behind the hills so the more elderly for whom the excitement of the day had proved too much, made their departures; but the bulk of us including the coach party remained, temporarily replete and talkative. Two hours later Maria Micri now dazed but still in her finery was still doing laps of honour in her grandmother's arms, her mother and father continued to respond to the cries of 'may the child live' and insatiable children and others who had got their second wind, took in fresh supplies of food and liquor. And as the stars came out and the lights went on and Klimi and Lukas sweated and served, so the evening grew more noisy and the children out of control. They fought and played among the tables and teased the cats who waited for scraps and did other dreadful things. One climbed a tree and fell from it into the laps of two widows deep in open-kneed conversation beneath it, another slipped his ice cream down his sister's back and a third, egged on by a little girl with bows in her hair, posted the remains of some fried fish through the driver's window of a Datsun. Mercifully for Klimi, from whom the mantle of geniality was falling fast, shortly after that exhibition of bravado the coach driver honked his horn and the rejoicings came to a close. Those children still engaged in combat were torn apart, bottoms were

smacked and faces washed and the company departed for
Rhodes in a mixture of tears, cheers and jollification. A
sleeping Maria Micri, her parents and her godfather
followed suit, the owner of the Datsun said his goodbyes,
and ushering his family into the saloon and seemingly
oblivious of the smell of fish, settled himself heavily into
his seat and drove happily away.

Klimi and Maria stood together and waved after them.
The brake lights glowed red as the car halted at the main
road and then vanished as it turned right. Gradually the
engine noise faded and the two of them walked slowly
back towards the taverna. For once neither of them was
bickering but their ebullience had evaporated and with the
passing of the limelight from her, Maria's hypochondria
had returned. She was, she announced, far from well and
was going to bed. Klimi glared after her retreating figure
and felt his face. 'Huh!' he said; and went inside to sulk
behind the counter. From the kitchen came the clattering
of plates as Lukas and Pavlos collected and presented
Katrina with dirty crockery and helped her with the
washing of them; and on the table by the door the cassette
player came to the end of a tape and clicked itself off.

'My oath,' said Pavlos addressing me as he appeared
from the kitchen and carrying his supper, 'it's gone like a
bloody morgue.' He repeated the statement in Greek to
Baba Yanni and Christos who were sitting with me and set
his plate on the table. 'Ne' they agreed, 'it is now very
quiet.' 'And also,' said Baba Yanni, 'it is still quite early.'
'Perhaps,' suggested Christos rising and crossing to the
cassette player and reversing the tape, 'we should have
some more music.' 'And perhaps,' called Baba Yanni who
showed no signs of opting for an early bedtime, 'we should
have another bottle?' 'And perhaps,' shouted a voice from

the periphery of the verandah, 'we should have another *two* bottles!' And in walked Bugs Bunny. Clearly it was not his first port of call.

'I have,' he advised us unnecessarily as he joined us at the table, 'had a little ouzo this evening.' 'Too right he has,' said Pavlos in an aside to me and handing him a chip, 'he's pissed.' 'Epharisto,' said Bugs Bunny, holding it like a cigarette; and nodded solemnly to each of us in turn. 'I have,' he continued, 'been with Panayotis.'

'Ah,' said Baba Yanni, 'was his stomach bad again?' 'Very,' said Bugs Bunny, and stubbed the chip into the ashtray. 'He was not, you understand, invited to the christening. And nor,' he added sourly, 'was I.'

Christos cleared his throat. 'Perhaps,' he advanced, 'it was unwise of you to have laughed at Klimi when he was bitten by the dog.' 'And perhaps,' said Baba Yanni, 'it was imprudent of you to have told the papas that the priests have too much power and too much money.' 'And also,' interposed Pavlos contributing to the post mortem, 'it was stupid to have told Katrina that Maria's moussaka was not as good as your wife's.' 'Ne,' agreed the others, 'perhaps if you had not said these certain things you *would* have been at the christening.'

Bugs Bunny blinked at them. 'Ah well,' he said philosophically, 'thenbarazi!' and drained his glass.

By ten o'clock he had emptied several more and his temper was more certain. Unfortunately his coordination was less so.

'Yanni mu,' I said, taking in the condition of his seventy years, 'let me walk home with you.' Yanni mu,' he said, rising unsteadily, 'why not?' And bidding goodnight to the others we walked back to his house at the top of the village. Unbelievably on the gateway was a Bunny Club sticker. It could have been his coat of arms.

Bugs Bunny looked at it in the porch light and patted it. 'Ine kala, ne?' he asked approvingly. 'America Booni Cloob.' 'Very beautiful,' I said, and followed him into the house.

We entered a huge room furnished with a single bed and one chair, countless fading photographs of fussily dressed children superimposed against crude backgrounds of hollyhocks and roses; and a very fat cat. Yellow eyed and black and with enormous whiskers it sat on the bed and mewed as its master approached.

'Ah,' said Bugs Bunny, gathering the obesity into his arms and hugging it, 'this is Moosi. He is, you understand, my very great friend. And these,' he said, gently replacing the monster on the bed and gesturing towards the picture gallery, 'are my family. And now Yanni, what will you drink?' 'Nothing,' I said holding up my hands, 'I must go.' 'Endaxi,' said Bugs Bunny, and took me to the door and out into the courtyard.

'Kalinichta Yanni,' he said, preparing to embrace me; and then stopped. 'Ah!' he said, 'I nearly forgot! One minute!' And pressing a light switch on the outside wall of another room, he flung open the door.

From high on a bunk a bundle of blankets galvanized into action, screamed, and fell to the floor. Bugs Bunny slammed the door shut and switched off the light. 'And that,' he said, 'was the wife. Kalinichta.'

Two weeks later I bade farewell to Bugs Bunny, and Gennadi. He came with others in the early afternoon to see me into the taxi which was to carry me to Rhodes, and to wish me a safe journey. And when I could see them no longer through the rear window of the car, I was sad; but I

'This is Moosi, my very great friend.'

took more than their good wishes with me on that day.

Between the leaves of my diary was the faded blue and green feather of the roller bird with which the young child Yanni had played and stroked my face. He had thrust it towards me that morning when I bent down to say goodbye to him on my last walk through the village. 'Take it,' said his mother. 'It is of course nothing you understand but it means much to him and he wishes you to have it.'

I still have that feather. Wrapped in tissue paper it lies in a drawer in my study desk together with a miscellany of bric-a-brac from Greece. Therein is the amber-coloured kombouloi, the worry beads which old Vasili gave to me the year before he died; the painted Paschal pullet's egg from a long past Easter in Kardamena, a red-veined trumpet shell from Fortula in Karpathos and the cheap key-ring of Evangelos which he pressed on me when first we met upon that island. There is the christening doll of Maria Micri, still filled with sugared almonds, the onyx pendant which the bearded Tito took from his neck and hung about my own the night we sang the song of Crete, and a lime-green stone washed smooth by the sea which I picked up and pocketed, the day the rabbit ran.

Collectively their intrinsic value is negligible but every object is a gem to me. Each is a memory bank which opens when I touch it and once again I feel the pulse of Greece and hear the heartbeat of the islands.

Back come the remembrances. Of scents of wild herbs in purple hills and Greek tobacco smoke and garlic; of sounds of hunting owls and braying mules and ubiquitous bouzoukois; of simple people with great hearts and inborn generosity; and of days, glorious, mercurial days of deep emotion and high elation when laughter swiftly turned to tears which just as quickly dried—the traits which are the very essence of the Greeks.

Such are the immortalities these trinkets hold. From them has grown this book. And through them my life has been immeasurably enriched—by the islanders of Greece. With them I have learned to live. And among them, I hope to end my days.

EBDON'S ODYSSEY
John Ebdon

A chance encounter set John Ebdon on a single-handed expedition to the Cyclades. There he fell irretrievably in love with the country, the island people and their way of life.

This brilliant, often very funny, account of his adventures on the islands of Andros and Kos is concerned with people, primarily the men and women of two villages on the islands but also with fellow countrymen who blundered into his life there.

'Any visitor to the Greek Islands will savour this account of the villages of Andros and Kos'
Sunday Telegraph

'anyone going in that direction (and those who have been) should read Mr Ebdon. In a sense his account is as highly coloured as any travel brochure, but, at least his picture is of real people and actual surroundings'.
Daily Telegraph

THE TIGRIS EXPEDITION
Thor Heyerdahl

Thor Heyerdahl's *Tigris* adventure began in the Garden of Eden on the bank of a river that flows from Ararat, where Noah's legendary ark once came to rest. It took him and his companions from nine nations in search of sea routes which he was sure must have been used by the ancient Sumerians 5,000 years ago on vessels like his own. His voyage down the Tigris, through the Gulf and eventually the Indian Ocean led to many discoveries and included many hazards. Modern shipping, bandits, reefs, and politics dogged *The Tigris Expedition*. Finally with permission to land only in the tiny republic of Djibouti and unable to continue the voyage for political reasons, *Tigris* was ceremonially burnt in protest against the intervention of major powers in African disputes which resulted in death and misery for millions of local people.

'The descriptive writing is as always good – the storms at sea; the pirates who demand exorbitant sums to haul them off the mud flats; and the excitement of playing with the sea creatures'.

Daily Telegraph

'a fascinating story of enterprise, history and adventure . . . backed by beautiful illustrations'.

Financial Times

THE KON-TIKI EXPEDITION
Thor Heyerdahl

The Kon-Tiki Expedition, which has sold several million copies, is an enthralling adventure story which tells how six young men defied expert advice and crossed the Pacific on a balsa-wood raft to test a theory.

'an incredible adventure which happens to be true'
> *SOMERSET MAUGHAM*

'an enthralling account of an experience without parallel'
> *RICHARD HUGHES*

'a bizarre and adventurous enterprise, excitingly and modestly recounted'
> *MALCOLM MUGGERIDGE*

BORN IN TIBET
Chögyam Trungpa

Born in Tibet tells the vivid story of the early life and
escape from Tibet of an incarnate lama of high rank. It
includes a fascinating account of the author's religious
education and the way of life of Tibet before the
Communist take-over. When the people rebelled
against the Chinese Communists, Trungpa Tulku
began a journey which led him eventually to India. His
escape makes a story which is both exciting and
moving, but throughout the book there is a thread of
compassion, for Trungpa Tulku can bear no hatred for
those who set out to destroy the Tibetan faith and way
of life.

'A delight and an eye-opener to the real life of a
Tibetan monk and the difficulties he endured in his
flight from the destroying Chinese invaders'.
Middle Way

'Deeply moving document . . . a sense of humour and
great courage seeps through this experience'.
Science of Thought Review

Also in Unwin Paperbacks

Ebdon's Odyssey *John Ebdon*	£2.50 ☐
The Tigris Expedition *Thor Heyerdahl*	£2.95 ☐
The Kon-Tiki Expedition *Thor Heyerdahl*	£1.95 ☐
Born in Tibet *Chogyam Trungpa*	£2.25 ☐

All these books are available at your local bookshop or newsagent, or can be ordered direct by post. Just tick the titles you want and fill in the form below.

Name ....

Address..

....

....

Write to Unwin Cash Sales, PO Box 11, Falmouth, Cornwall TR10 9EN.

Please enclose remittance to the value of the cover price plus:

UK: 50p for the first book plus 20p for the second book, thereafter 14p for each additional book ordered, to a maximum charge of £1.68.

BFPO and EIRE: 50p for the first book plus 20p for the second book and 14p for the next 7 books and thereafter 8p per book.

OVERSEAS: 85p for the first book plus 23p per copy for each additional book.

Unwin Paperbacks reserve the right to show new retail prices on covers, which may differ from those previously advertised in the text or elsewhere. Postage rates are also subject to revision.